Praise for Jazzman

"*Jazzman* is the vivid tale of Lance Willliams, a brilliant, innovative and troubled trumpet player in a golden age of jazz in the '40s and '50s, back when such musicians as John Coltrane and Charlie Mingus were household names. Mr. Fogg, a veteran novelist and former corporate executive and consultant, is himself a former jazz musician. He has long known that world inside and out.

"The novel takes us from Lance's prodigy years as a youth in Buffalo to fame and then decline, to near self-destruction, from drug addiction, amidst the stresses and temptations of the capital of jazz -- New York City -- and then back to his provincial but welcoming hometown as he tries to put his life together again. Along the way we get an unforgettable insider's look at the smoky world of jazz -- that great American art form - and a panoramic view of churning mid-century life."

-Robert Whitcomb, Opinion page editor, *Providence Journal*

"When it comes to writing about jazz and jazz musicians, Dave Fogg really knows the territory. Having co-fronted a working jazz quintet with him many years ago, I can vouch for his fine musicianship. And as for the quality of his writing, this book speaks for itself. Read it, and be transported to the smoked filled jazz clubs of the nascent bop era, and hear its music as you follow the roller coaster career of Dave's trumpet-playing protagonist."

-David Shire, Icon in Hollywood and on Broadway

Publisher's Information

EBookBakery Books

Author contact: davis.fogg@gmail.com

ISBN: 978-1-953080-05-9

Library of Congress Control Number:

1. Jazz 2. Miles Davis 3. Jazz History 4. Music

© 2020 by C. Davis Fogg

ALL RIGHTS RESERVED
No part of this work covered by the copyright herein may be reproduced, transmitted, stored, or used in any form or by any means graphic, electronic, or mechanical, including but not limited to photocopying, scanning, digitizing, taping, Web distribution, information networks, or information storage and retrieval systems, except as permitted by Section 107 or 108 of the 1976 United States Copyright Act, without the prior written permission of the author.

This is a work of fiction
Some, but not all of the dialogue and descriptions are fictional.
The characters are real.

DEDICATION

For Kate: My Love, My Muse, My Life

JAZZMAN

C. DAVIS FOGG

CONTENTS

THE BEGINNINGS 1
SENIOR PROM 7
ACCOLADES 13
JULLIARD 17
THE BIG BREAK 21
THE STUDIO 25
IMPROVISATION 29
THE INTERVIEW 35
MINGUS AND LANCE 41
RECKONING 45
THE APOLLO THEATER 47
OVERDOSE 53
HOSPITAL 57
DETOX AND RECOVERY 61
TRAIN TO BUFFALO 67
HOME 71
BRUCKNER'S 73
JOB HUNT 77
IN LIMBO 79
TRAIN TO NEW YORK 81
ABOUT THE AUTHOR 85

1
The Beginnings

IN EARLY MAY OF 1955, Lance Williams stood on the stage at the Village Vanguard in New York, one of the world's top temples of jazz, where only the best headlined. He wore his usual all-black garb—T-shirt, jeans, leather jacket, and metal-trimmed biker boots. Painted by the pale-yellow spotlight that made his brass trumpet sparkle like golden jewelry, Williams stared out at the rabid jazz fans through a haze of eye-stinging blue smoke. He ignored the low chatter and clink of ice cubes in glasses, and the whirr of a blender in the background. Lance leaned back slightly as if an invisible hand was gently pressing on his chest, and pointed his trumpet straight at the audience. The spotlight played his moving silhouette on the wall at the back of the stage. It was as if a large shadowy ghost was mimicking his movements. *Well here goes. You'd better swing tonight man. The reviewers from Downbeat and the Times are here to catch the first night of the show. Scary.*

Max Roach, leader of the quintet, jazz star, and future Jazz Hall of Famer, counted off four beats. John Coltrane, recognized as the best tenor sax man in the world, played the introductory chorus. Then Lance blew a sizzling solo on Dizzy Gillespie's classic "A Night in Tunisia." The tempo was breakneck. The solo lofted like a hawk in flight, soaring and maneuvering on currents, twisting and turning with the beat. He negotiated vast intervals, rapid tonging, soaring arpeggios, with a round and dark tone. He brought the audience with him on his emotional flights. He took his bow to great and sustained applause, and thought: *Maybe the critics' buzz is right. Maybe I'm on the verge of joining the ranks of stars like Miles (Davis), Dizzy (Gillespie), and Brownie (Clifford Brown).*

Lance loved his audiences—young adults, college kids, ardent jazz fans, and other musicians there to see what was happening in vibrant, sometimes shocking, and evolving modern jazz. There were other fans of the jazz scene—older people graduating from Dixieland and big swing bands and the curious "early adopters." They were the people that caught the new modern sounds, the virtuosity and the freedom of the soul that improvised jazz provided. Followers could disappear into "the groove" and forget everything around them and the outside world.

At three, Lance Williams startled his parents by singing, in his high, little-boy voice, or humming songs that he heard his father play on the piano, or from jazz and classical records constantly being played in their modest home. His father, Sam, was a piano teacher and jazz-dance bandleader, and well suited to teach Lance how to play the piano.

At four, with his father's instruction, and before his rebellion, Lance would play the piano sitting on three thick telephone directories stacked on the piano bench so he could reach the keys. His pudgy legs dangled over the seat, and his sneakered feet could not yet reach the pedals. He could play basic jazz and classical pieces without music. His rhythm and chords were dead-on and he added a few flourishes of his own. No simplistic starter student pieces like "Row, Row, Row Your Boat" for him.

Lance had perfect pitch, a rarity. He could identify the exact pitch of a note no matter who was playing it. When practicing and performing, he would hit every note perfectly. Soon, he could play moderately difficult chords and classical works such as Beethoven's "Minuet in G." Not perfectly, but the basics were in place. His style had lilt, crisp phrasing, sharp tonguing, unique interpretation and, most of all, fire. He began playing jazz tunes that he heard from his father's record collection. His favorite jazz pianist was Art Tatum, considered the greatest jazz pianist of all time. His classical hero was pianist Vladimir Horowitz, whose bombastic style perfectly interpreted Rachmaninoff. Lance loved bombastic.

Totally focused, Lance enveloped himself in his musical cocoon. He was oblivious to anything from the outside world that threatened to intrude on his magical times. He felt a wash of warmth and excitement come over him every time he played. It was if the music had been specifically written for him.

By five, Lance was playing difficult classical pieces including Beethoven's "Minuet in C," and Chopin's mazurkas. The speedy rondo of the Chopin piece was made for Lance's facile playing. He caressed the keys;

he felt the music and the composer's intent. He started composing full-fledged Mozart-like pieces.

One day his father said, "Lance, how would you like to go with me to our gig tomorrow night—big seventeen-piece band? My best. Formal affair, you'll have to dress up smart—long pants, your best shirt, and your good shoes. It's at the Century Association Time to see all of the swells that pay our bills."

Excited, Lance said, "Sure Dad!"

"Great. We'll leave after dinner."

Lance was in awe of the whole scene. He felt almost an adult. Enthralled. There were men in tuxes who looked like huge penguins. The women, in fancy ball gowns and cocktail dresses of every shade of the rainbow, looked like cotton candy with legs. Flowers and candles decorated every table. Waiters in black tails were busy serving meals, a curious novelty for him. Mom always served their meals, except when they went to a hotdog-polish sausage joint for a charcoal-grilled treat. Being from a middle-class family, he was puzzled; intrigued.

Lance's legs bounced with the rhythm, and he unconsciously played the band's chords with his fingers just as he would on a piano. He tingled. He was mesmerized. He was sucked into the vortex of a new musical experience. The jazz music became his heart and soul. He was hooked.

Lance loved the trumpets. The shiny brass instruments caught his fancy. The four horns seemed to fly over the ensemble, brilliant in tone, fast and fluid in their playing. And they did amazing improvised solos and played mellow and sultry ballads. He thought, *I want to play the trumpet. I want to stand up and play jazz. I hate the piano.*

When the band broke to pack up, Lance went up to the first trumpet, Tony Cavallaro and said, "You sounded great. Can I hold your horn?" The trumpet player reluctantly handed the expensive custom-made horn to Lance and showed him how to hold it. Normally Cavalaro wouldn't let anyone so much as touch his ax. *The kid's the boss's son so I don't really have much choice. If he drops the horn, I'll kill him.*

Lance carefully took the instrument in his hands, put his lips to the mouthpiece, and blew hard. Out came a sound as wild as an elephant's bray and a jackass's he-haw. Tony laughed hard, and said, "That's really, really bad. Let me show you how it works. By the way, it takes a long, long

THE BEGINNINGS

time for a student to get a steady decent tone, and a few thousand hours of practicing to get good and play like the boys in the band—ten thousand to become superb and as good as anyone on the circuit. You have to build up your face and lip muscles and breath.

Lance said, "I'll practice all day long if I can get as good as you."

Tony advised, "Put your lips together and take a deep breath into your stomach. Then pucker your lips slightly, like this, and blow out as if you're trying to hit the wall over there with your wind. Don't press hard. That will only louse you up. Put as little pressure as possible on the mouthpiece." Tony patted Lance's stomach and said: "Breathe from your diaphragm. Your stomach should expand and then contract as you push air through the horn." Lance tried a few times, and Cavallaro showed him where to place the mouthpiece on his lips. "Now flick your tongue to start the airflow and gently blow *through* the horn at the wall."

Lance blew a steady stream of air this time and produced a wobbly but credible middle C. Tony moved the trumpet's valves up and down, producing a precarious "Twinkle Little Star." "Great," the Cavallero said. "You're a natural. You should take up the trumpet."

Pleased and thrilled, Lance beamed. "But I play the piano and Dad will be mad if I switch instruments."

"Ask him if you can play both."

"No. I want to play the trumpet."

"This is up to you and your Dad."

The day after the dance, angry and showing his soon-to-be legendary temper, Lance stomped into the music room in his house for his daily lesson, walked to the piano, slammed down the keyboard cover, and refused to play. Sulking, his arms folded over his chest, red-faced, he glowered petulantly at his father.

"No way! I want to play trumpet. I hate the piano! I hate you. No more piano. No more lessons. I want to play in your band."

"You have to play piano. You're a prodigy. You can be a top-ranked concert pianist—play with the major symphonies throughout the world."

"No. I won't," Lance yelled as he swept a pile of music onto the floor. "I want to play jazz."

Angrily and forcefully his father took his arm and pushed him toward the piano. "Lance, get up on the stool and practice." Lance broke away and barged out of the room into his bedroom, slamming the door with a window-rattling bang.

Spoiled rotten, Lance most always got his way. A few days later, reluctantly, and with the admonition that he must continue with the piano, his father bought Lance a low-priced student trumpet that was adequate for Lance's early days. It was well used, dented in a few places, and the brilliant lacquer had been rubbed off the brass in places. It was more suited for a marching band than a concert hall and yielded an unexceptional tone. Sluggish valves limited his facility in getting around the horn, making fast runs difficult. The instrument did not produce the rich, round tone so valued by trumpeters. He stubbornly refused to take piano lessons after that, despite the frequent entreaties that he continue both. His parents gave up after a while.

Lance almost wore out his father's records of the best big bands and small groups of the times—Stan Kenton, Duke Ellington, and Harry James were his favorites. He listened to the best small groups—John Coltrane, Miles Davis, and Max Roach. His favorite trumpet players were the best of the best—Louis Armstrong, Clark Terry, Clifford Brown, and Dizzy Gillespie.

His father signed Lance up for classical trumpet lessons at the Buffalo School of Music. Tony Cavallero taught him jazz. By eight, he could play some of the very difficult classical pieces such as Paganini's "Moto Perpetuo," and Giannini's "Concerto in B-Flat for Trumpet." He could play and improvise jazz like a pro. By ten he was sitting in or playing with his father's band and taking other jobs with big bands, polka groups, and small jazz ensembles. His gigs were illegal because he was under age, but the Musician's Union and members of the bands that he played with protected him.

His gigs with big bands, and particularly small groups, let Lance use his vast inbred talents for improvisation. Improvisation is a skill that can't be taught. With inbred talent, it is relatively easy, and is honed by playing with and listening to others. At twelve, he formed his own quintet under the tutelage of his father, and played a lot of high school dance dates throughout the city. At fourteen he became the go-to guy for first trumpet in amateur big bands, and the lead voice in small groups.

Jazz became his life.

When they were both eleven and in fifth grade, Lance and Denny Cole, son of their school music teacher and one of Lance's best friends, stood sweaty and apprehensive under the lights of a TV studio in downtown Philadelphia. Denny's father, Sam, had heard through the grapevine that Paul Whitman, a famous bandleader and television personality, was holding auditions for his popular TV Teen Club. Whitman's intention was to highlight very talented teenagers. Sam drove them to the TV studio.

Lance and Denny had watched a parade of hopefuls perform—dancers in cute costumes, singers, jugglers, piano players, and a stand-up comedian who told kiddie jokes, among others. Stage mothers were ever present. Lance and Denny played a duet, "Tea for Two," a cute, rather basic piece, but a staple in the repertoire of young students. Surprisingly, they thought, they were selected for the show. A show composer did an arrangement for the duo with the Whitman band. Then they returned to the studio to play the real thing. Their performance was flawless, in spite of a severe case of nerves. They both reveled in the attention that they got under the spotlight and the applause from the studio audience.

Lance felt the thrill of attention. He felt grown up. *Look at me*, he thought. *I'm special. Really good. Everyone will be impressed.* One of the producers approached Lance after the session and said, "You're talented. Here's my card. Come and see me in a year or so when you've developed a bit more. Maybe I can help you. There are lots of TV shows and concerts that feature soloists like you." Lance and Denny went home floating on clouds of shimmering music.

2

SENIOR PROM

IN MAY OF 1948, Lance's big band was playing for the senior prom in Madison High School's gym. The dance was a big deal for the seniors. Even more so for Lance. He could show off in front of his peers and teachers.

He fielded a seventeen-piece jazz band made up of the most talented high school jazz-dance musicians in Western New York and supplemented by three pros to bolster up the weak spots. The band had four trumpets, five saxes, three trombones, piano, and an acoustic bass who doubled on electric bass drums and Latin percussion. One trumpet was a screamer who could navigate the highest notes on the horn and improvise like hell—as good as Maynard Ferguson from Kenton's band. Lance had bandstands, blue with large letters that spelled out LW, and with lights that illuminated the music without intruding on the sometimes-dreamy mood on the dance floor. He had an expensive book of over fifty pieces that he had purchased. It included a raft of styles—swing, jitterbug, jazz, ballads, rock, and all kinds of Latin music. These necessities were paid for from his now-substantial earnings from his many gigs. Lance's band was well-rehearsed and the best big band in the Buffalo area, professional bands included.

Lance and his girlfriend, Martha, went into the Madison High School gym an hour before the dance was to begin so they could set up the bandstand, put out the music and playlist for the dance, and test the PA system.

The theme of the dance was "My Romance," and versions of the song by Doris Day, Sarah Vaughn, and Frank Sinatra would be played during all the band's breaks.

When they got to the gym, Lance and Martha entered a festive space with red crepe paper intertwined with sparkling silver strands streaming from the light fixtures and basketball nets. An abundance of red and white roses in large vases stood in front of the band and presentation stage. Hanging beside the stage were four, five-foot red satin hearts surrounded by thick layers of white organza, and punctured by golden arrows. Two large cupids with their love-strung bows and arrows loomed over the stage. Royal purple chairs awaited the prom king and queen. A massive projection screen on one side-wall played ever-changing romantic scenes of Hollywood stars, such as Lana Turner and Clark Gable in *Homecoming*.

"Wow, what a sendoff for our class," Martha said. "But it's sad. We won't see many of our friends after graduation. They're scattering all over the country."

"Too bad," Lance said, "but we'll be in touch with some of our best friends. I'll be at Juilliard, and there will be some of the gang in the New York area that I can see."

"What about us Lance? I'll be at Stanford. We can't afford to get together during the school year."

"We can write to each other, have the occasional phone call—too expensive to call a lot, but we'll be together during vacations."

Lance took her in his arms, kissed her, and said, "I love you. We'll find a way."

Martha gave him big hug and they set about their work.

Martha arranged the band's music stands and set out the night's music. Lance went about testing the piano and sound system.

"Christ, Martha," Lance said in disdain, "look at this pathetic piano. Scratched, dented, and carved initials all over the damn thing. The keys are so grubby that you'd have to scrape the gunk off to see the fake ivories. Looks like the battered beer-soaked piano that Dooley Wilson played in *Casablanca*."

"Never heard of him." Martha said.

Lance played Carmichael's "I Get Along Without You Very Well," and added, "People don't know how famous he was. He wrote dozens of songs for Broadway, TV, and film. He wrote spectacular ballads including "Stardust," "The Nearness of You," and "Skylark," to name a few. Listen, the piano is in tune. I badgered the school to get it fixed, probably for the first time in years."

Lance, who doubled as MC for the affair, set about testing the school's rickety-squeaky sound system. It projected static and crackles. It was useless to amplify the band, and he decided to use it only for announcements. The powerful band needed no amplification and they weren't using a singer who would need a good system.

The band members began to straggle in, greeted each other, took their places, and started the cacophony of warming up and practicing a few of the more difficult charts.

Just before the downbeat for the first dance, Louis Jordan's "Saturday Night Fish Fry," Martha's eyes twinkled, and a with wry look on her face she joked, "Now Lance, keep your ogles off the sexy girls and scope me. I'm the only woman that you can look at. Just think of the challenge of getting under my poofy petticoats later."

Lance responded, "Absolutely no problem. How about a roll in the sand at Shirkston Beach? Everyone's going there after the dance, and there are plenty of sand dunes where we can spread a blanket and make whoopee without being seen."

"Oooo. Can't wait. I'm horny as hell, and wet just thinking about it." And, she added with a puckish look, "I'll be your ever-faithful 'band widow'. I'll sit beside the band like a wallflower—silent, unobtrusive, demure, and basking in the Champagne light thrown off by your stunning self."

Lance chucked. "Yeah, sure, you bettcha. Just be your usual sexy self and our first ballad will be our song: "I Only Have Eyes for You." By the way, be sure to keep your eyes off hot men out there."

"Maybe" Martha said with sassy a smile and raised eyebrows.

It was a foregone conclusion that the prom queen would be Sandra Ensminger, the most beautiful girl in the class. She was a brainy, platinum-haired cheerleader who looked a little bit like Carole Lombard. Sandra would be draped with a golden-edged red sash, and crowned with a bright, large, fake gold tiara gushing rhinestones.

Frank Fischer, Sandra's steady, would be king. He was Italian and looked like a rugged Mario Lanza, a movie swoon of the day. Lots of girls cast approving and wishful eyes on Frank; teenage infatuation it was. He only got a small dully decorated silver orb, and a narrow red sash with no sparkling trim—arranged by the prom committee which was all female.

But the king was window dressing for the queen. She was short, he a handsome muscular 6'3" star basketball player. They were an inseparable couple—a true Mutt and Jeff. Some said that they were headed for marriage. Rumor had it that they had "done it." Their fine jitterbugging and bop dancing put icing on the cake.

The dress was par for the course for a prom. The girls-come-women wore light-colored chiffon ball gowns, or shorter cocktail dresses with pastels preferred—blue, purple, green and pink, and the old standbys, white and black. Many purloined their mother's jewelry and uncomfortable high heels, which streamlined and showed off their legs. There was an occasional teasing glimpse of panties when they twirled. Sexy, they and the boys thought. The girls were wearing the inevitable wrist corsages—usually fragrant gardenias, or the occasional orchid that boys scrimped for. More likely, that the parents paid for.

The boy-men were dashing and a little awkward in their rented white dinner jackets with tux pants. A number sported black patent leather dancing shoes—called "fairy" shoes by some. A few daring boys wore red dinner jackets and ruffed shirts. The rented magic was due back at the store on Monday—a task that parents were likely to be burdened with.

After the band started playing, Martha had a cup of teenager appropriate non-alcoholic, bilious fruit punch dipped from a bowl floating with misty dry ice, lemon, and orange slices. The class clown and hell-raiser spiked the punch with vodka halfway through the affair. Better refreshments—beer and hard liquor—were already secreted in cars or on the grounds for access during the dance, usually accompanying world class necking or fucking.

There were the ever-present teachers and parent chaperones all over the place. They were to watch for too-close dancing and other misbehaviors. Halfway through the prom, high on their own liquor stashes, they didn't give a much of a damn what happened.

Lance played the lush, sensual ballads: "Tenderly," "Over the Rainbow," and "P.S. I Love You." Rock dancing ceased, and the crowd slipped into slow, barely moving motion, with eyes closed, arms around each other, and deep kissing. You couldn't get a piece of paper between any of them.

It was a crowning night for Lance. He stood out in front of the crowd and showed how good he was. Faculty congratulated him. Many students came up to talk to him. He was high—especially about the bevy of girls that seemed to be attracted to him.

Martha and Lance packed up the band gear and hurried outdoors for their drive to Shirkston beach. The rest of the revelers who were going there had a head start. Nonetheless, they would find a private dune that they could have all to themselves.

There was little traffic on the Peace Bridge between Buffalo and Canada. After they got over the bridge and into Ontario Province, they turned left onto the narrow, almost-deserted shore road to Shirkston just a few miles away. Martha immediately pulled down her dress top and bra, exposing her "two-handful" breasts, topped by luscious pink nipples which were blood-gorged. Lance had a "necker knob" on his steering wheel, so that he could easily steer the car with one hand. He moved his hand to Martha's breasts, and gently massaged them. Martha moved her hand up and down Lance's thigh, occasionally massaging his crotch, but careful not to get him off. That was the first order of business when they settled onto the beach.

The edge of the beach was dotted mostly with empty cars—a few with steamed-up windows masking predictable motions inside. Lance was careful to park the car on solid ground. Every year, some fools parked on the sand and had to have their car towed. There would be hell to pay when their parents got the bill for that little mistake.

Martha and Lance threw off their shoes, grabbed a blanket and a bag with beer, and hurried to the edge of the expanse. Sounds of laughter, conversations, and the unmistakable utterances of sweet talk and sex drifted over the dunes. Lance said, with a smile, "Things are well underway. We have a lot of catching up to do."

Martha responded, "I've been wet and ready since the Peace Bridge."

The beach was bathed in the magical glow of bluish-white light from a three-quarters moon. The frothing edges of mild breakers glowed with the moon's pervasive light. The sound of the breakers provided a throbbing rhythm for fervent lovemaking.

Lance and Martha wended their way between dunes, sneaking looks into the nests of laughing, drinking, singing, talking, intertwined couples. Unbelievably, they found, unoccupied, their usual spot, with three high deep sides and one partially open to the ocean and covered by sea grass. They could not be seen unless someone tumbled over the side of their nest—a slight, but real possibility.

They foot-skied down a side of the dune, and crumbled into the bottom, laughing and covered with sand. They hurriedly stood up and spread out the blanked. Washed with love, Martha and Lance stood facing each other. Lance helped Martha out of her sand-laden gown which slithered, along with her underwear, into a heap at her feet. She undressed Lance, removing his tented shorts, and they lay down and made love. Then made love again. Spent, they turned over and stared up at the winking bright stars, which seemed as if they were beaming only for them.

Martha said, "We'll be together forever."

Lance took her in his arms once more, cuddled her, deeply kissed her, and said, "Yes." Little did they know that, after summer vacation, they wouldn't see each other for years;

3
ACCOLADES

THE ACCOLADES FLOWED. LANCE was asked to play first trumpet in the Buffalo Philharmonic during a rehearsal under the storied conductor Joseph Krips, formerly conductor of the Vienna State Opera orchestra and the Vienna Symphony. He was awestruck walking into the Symphony's home, Kleinhan's Music Hall. It had 2,800 red plush seats placed in rows curving from one side of the hall to the other. And the acoustics were excellent, something that could not be said about the homes of a lot of orchestras. No one, as hard as they tried, could match the sound of Carnegie Hall, the gold standard of orchestral homes. Lance could imagine it filled with a sea of classical music lovers chatting and laughing, waiting for the conductor to walk on stage, acknowledge the applause, and step up on the podium. Many of the musicians were on stage chatting with colleagues or warming up with a babble of scales, arpeggios, and excerpts from the music to be rehearsed. Occasionally someone played a hot jazz lick or part of a popular hit song.

Lance walked on the stage to the trumpet section and sat down next to Joe Manisco, the orchestra's principal trumpet. They were to play "Der Meistersinger," which had one of the most challenging trumpet parts in the orchestral spectrum. Lance's remarkable solo was a powerful flight that soared above the orchestra and stated the main theme of the opera. Lance had already rehearsed the piece so thoroughly with his teacher and mentor, Gene Bishop, that he could play it in his sleep.

Manisco coached him on how Krips conducted. "He is precise as a metronome and you have to watch him like a hawk. He barely moves his baton except when he wants to change the dynamic or cue in a solo or section, then he's a bit more direct and effusive. When he indicates that you're to come in, he'll stare straight at you, drilling bullets into your eyes just before you're to come in." Krips was authoritarian old-school Germanic conductor who always wore a custom-made, immaculately-pressed black suit that could wrap around his considerable girth to rehearsal. He looked like a Prussian general sternly leading his troops into battle.

During the rehearsal, a flute player literally and figuratively blew it. The orchestra was playing a soft pianissimo section when the player absent-mindedly jumped into the next section of the piece, a loud fast-tempoed scherzo. Instead of dealing pleasantly with the mistake, Krips turned red with anger, never looking at the player, and said to the orchestra manager, "I want to see that man in my office immediately after the rehearsal." That scared the hell out of Lance, lest he be the object of the conductor's wrath. He played like a pro.

After the rehearsal, Krips singled out Lance and moved toward him. *Fucking A*, Lance thought, almost quivering, and looking for a place to hide. *What in hell did I do wrong?* Though he rarely gave complements, Krips told Lance, "You play magnificently. All you need is experience and a good musical education."

"I've been thinking of going to Juilliard"

"With your talent you should. I'll write a recommendation for you."

Lance was puzzled when Krips handed him a card with several phone numbers and addresses, and Krips said, "I'm guest conductor at the Berlin Philharmonic, Milan Opera, the Chicago Symphony, and others, so I move around a lot." Indicating one number on the card he said, "Call this number in Berlin. My secretary can always put you in touch with me no matter where I am."

Surprised, Lance hesitated until he realized the import of Krip's offer, then said," Thank you, thank you," feeling slightly giddy and proud of himself. This just added to his big head and his feeling that he was a prima donna and performed better than any other trumpet player in the world.

The honors continued. Lance was solo cornet in the New York State band and first trumpet in the orchestra. He got top grades in competitions, and his only challenger was Fred Mills who went on to found the Canadian Brass. The *Buffalo Evening News* ran a front-page feature article on Lance as a prodigy student star. Contest judges and Tony Cavallero all encouraged him to go to the Juilliard after he graduated from high school. His parents wanted him to go if he could get a scholarship. Lance had no doubt that Juilliard would accept him and pay his way. *I'll be one of their most famous graduates.*

4
Juilliard

LANCE CAREFULLY PACKAGED A tape of difficult jazz and classical performances and references to send to send Juilliard with his application for an audition. He had stellar endorsements from Gene Bishop, his instructor, and Joseph Krips, conductor of the Buffalo Philharmonic. They thought he was a shoe-in.

Recommendations helped but were a minor factor to Juilliard in considering applicants' tryouts for their Jazz program. It was the audiotape of difficult classical and jazz pieces that should get him a hearing. The jazz selections, played by his big band and quintet, featured his fluid style and creative improvisation. There were lush ballads, driving fast pieces, some bebop, and others in mainstream modern jazz. To put icing on the cake, he soloed with his big band on his own up-tempo, hard-charging composition, "Martha," written for his high school sweetheart. He felt that it captured her bright, inquisitive and outgoing personality, and thought that Juilliard's admissions people would be impressed with his composition and arranging abilities.

After an excruciating wait, Lance received a letter from Juilliard inviting him to New York for a live audition. The date was January 18th, his birthday. *Christ, we'll probably have five feet of snow on the ground by then, and I'll leave in the middle of a blizzard no doubt. New York has to be more civilized than this burg.*

Lanced arrived at Grand Central Station after a rickety-clickity ride on the New York Central Line from Buffalo. Exiting the station, he was awed by the skyscrapers, the raucous horn-blowing traffic, and the hustle and bustle of ever-hurrying pedestrians. *I'll get my ass to Juilliard, then hit some jazz clubs and see the town later.* He took the subway to The Julliard School on Columbus Avenue and 64th and passed through the large marble plaza containing the three classical-modern buildings that housed the New York Philharmonic, Metropolitan Opera, and New York City Ballet.

Lance met the assigned second-year student who would guide him through registration and other things that he ought to see and do during his stay. He told Lance what his own audition was like, saying that he was very nervous before he played and a little skittish between numbers when the judges were privately discussing his playing. "I thought that I'd really screwed up, but after all I got in, so don't sweat it. You'll play far better than you think you did." *Shit never been nervous, never lost, and won't this time either.*

Lance moved into a minimally-furnished dormitory room that he would share with a Chinese cellist who barely spoke English and said little more than, "Hi "before he returned to studying a score. Lance was thankful. He needed his rest and quiet.

After dinner, Lance went into a practice room to rehearse rough spots in his pieces. The conflicting sounds of many instruments seeped into the hallways from other nearby rooms. He shut his door, blanked out the minor intrusions from the hall, and concentrated on his task. Satisfied with his rehearsal, he went back to his room and fell into a restless sleep. After he awoke, he went and had a light breakfast and mentally envisioned a perfect tryout.

Confidently sitting beside the door to the audition room, he heard the strains of a challenging violin concerto. Shortly, his wilted and discouraged-looking roommate, head down, cello case in hand, exited the room. *I guess he didn't do so well. Too bad. I'll knock 'em dead.*

When called, Lance walked into the audition room. There was a Steinway grand piano, and posters of famous musicians who had graduated from Juilliard lined the walls. Represented among the famous were Miles Davis, Tito Puente, Itzhak Perlman, and Richard Rodgers. Three stern-looking men sat at a table in deep discussion, still evaluating the merits of the exiting cellist. They scribbled a few notes on some papers, then stood up with welcoming smiles and said, in unison, "Lance, welcome to the best music conservatory in the world." They introduced themselves, and among them was the top jazz trumpet instructor, Joe Wilder, who was chairman of the jury.

Lance knew from a *Downbeat* article, sent in a literature pack from Juilliard, that Wilder had played with the who's who of band leaders—Dizzy

Gillespie, Count Basie, Gil Evans, and Jimmie Lunsford. He was in groups that backed up the ilk of Lena Horne, Tony Bennett, and Billie Holiday. He was much loved and was the first black to play in Broadway pit orchestras and the studio bands of radio and television. Quite a presence.

Lance was to play, in order, the required program so that the jury could easily compare candidates. He was to play the Hummel and Giannini trumpet concertos and a Ravel étude. The jazz numbers, which occupied most of the hour-and-a-quarter session, included slow, medium, and up-tempo compositions: Ellington's "Sophisticated Lady"; Kern/Hammerstein's "All the Things You Are"; Charlie Parker's "Confirmation"; and Buaza's "Mambo Inn." The pieces required every critical skill that a trumpeter would use—high and low register, extreme intervals, tone, and facility on slow and very fast passages, legato, and staccato. And most of all, the heart and soul of creative improvisation and interpretation.

Lance put his music on a stand, unpacked his trumpet, did a few warm-up scales, and then nodded to the judges that he was ready to play. He signaled his appointed piano accompanist to start the program.

The jury conferred among themselves between a few of the selections, scribbling notes but otherwise not interacting with Lance except to occasionally encourage him: "Very nice Lance; style is good; you're on the right track; go on; inventive improvisation." After he completed the program, Lance, flooded with the excited energy of a winning athlete thought, *Shit, perfect, couldn't be better. Wowed them. On my way. An obvious admit.*

The jury spent about five minutes discussing his performance and scribbling notes. *What the fuck,* Lance thought, *why so much time? I should be an obvious choice.* Then the jury members gave their comments:

Wilder said, "Fine overall technique and superb interpretation both on classical and jazz. Improvisation was spectacular, but you need a lot of work to become a real pro. You have issues. How were you trained?"

Lance explained, "Mostly public-school music teachers. Then in 7th and 8th grade, taught by instructors from the Curtis Conservatory in Philadelphia. But I quit after eighth grade."

"Why did you quit?"

"I was so good that there was little statewide competition. No reason to go on. I could sight-read and play anything superbly. Besides girls, my social life and dance and jazz gigs ate up a slew of time."

Another said, "Your experience in jazz is excellent. Forming two bands is a major accomplishment. But I see from your application that you've had little of the classical trumpet repertoire. It's important that you learn more classics. They're critical for your further developing and maintaining your skills."

The third judge inserted, "Your fast arpeggios are a bit uneven, and your very high notes are weak. With work, you can fix these problems. And you're leaking air from the right side of your mouthpiece. This is distracting to listeners and costs you power in your delivery. There are other fundamentals that need work. You need a complete tune-up to put you on par with the best students here. If you get in, you'll get pushed to the extreme." Lance was quiet, ashen, deflated and shocked. *Christ. Never ever had shitty comments like this before.*

Wilder closed the session by thanking Lance and told him that they would decide in about a month. When closing the door to the audition room, a jury member left the door cracked, so Lance put his ear to the opening and listened to the jury's comments.

He heard Wilder say, "May be a diamond in the rough. But he doesn't have the polish that most of our applicants have gained through years of instruction. I'd keep him in the pool when it comes to final selections, but if we select him, it will be based on raw talent and interpretation."

The other judges agreed.

Angry, crushed, and nauseous, Lance picked up his axe and music and headed for Grand Central and the trip back to Buffalo. A few minutes after the train left New York, emotionally drained and exhausted, he tried to take a nap. It didn't take. His "monkey brain," working at warp speed, kept him jittery and hyper. He headed to the bar car to get very, very drunk and tried to rationalize what just happened.

His visions of standing on the stage at the storied Vanguard and blowing the critics and audience away, dimmed.

5
The Big Break

IN HIS APARTMENT, LANCE slumped into a tattered Salvation Army chair. The rat-a-tat military cadence from tight-skinned snares and the thunderous boom of the bass drums screamed in his brain. He was agitated, depressed, and exhausted. He had contacted all the jazz musicians from his and Trombley's lists with little result. *Shit man,* he thought, *I've talked to mucho jazzmen, agents, and show people without getting much work—a few unimportant studio sessions backing second-tier singers and musicians. Clark Terry got me a job playing second trumpet in the pit of "Auntie Mame." A foot in the door, but way down the call list for future theater stints. The shit-eating dance and bar stuff barely pays the rent, food, and booze. The guys with the jobs don't think of me when the good stints come along. I keep calling my contacts almost to the point of annoyance. Not good.*

Lance went back to reading Jack Kerouac's *On the Road*. Kerouac was one of his heroes. The bohemian beatnik author stood for many of the things that Lance believed in. A counter-culture lifestyle. Freedom from society's establishment. Abundant drugs—pot, Benzedrine, peyote, heroin and LSD. A lot of other musicians thought that drugs and booze enhanced creativity and pushed their improvisation to new heights. He knew that drugs could lead to degeneration of their ability to play, physical decay, and even death.

Lance was aroused like a teenager in heat. The free love thing and visions of pot-fired promiscuous women dancing with flowered garlands in their hair and wearing see-through gossamer gowns, which they pulled up over their heads inviting sex on a whim or desire. Or dancing with a sexy guy, falling into the dude's arms, diving onto the mucky field, and joining a group fucking in the open.

Sometimes, on stage during a gig, a musician would sit out a number or two and have a prearranged quickie in the dark backstage or a secluded spot rarely visited.

A lot of people knew about these assignation spots which they avoided when the pew was occupied. Groupies often had the hots for trumpet players, and were aroused by hot pounding music, a seductive ballad, or just plain horniness. One woman, markedly high on something, stepped up to the stage during a sweet rendition of "Little Girl Blue," a plaintive Rogers and Hart ballad to be sung to an unhappy girl. The audience was silent, transported into their own private space. Maybe they were feeling empathy for a friend, lamenting a long-lost love, or just feeling the beautiful, romantic classic song.

In the middle of the tune, a young, startlingly beautiful, drug-high redhead rushed to the stage. She had Julianna Moore's "fuck me" look, and the actor's penchant for having nude and very explicit, athletic, sex scenes in her movies. The woman bared her ample and bouncy breasts, gave Lance a blood-red magic marker and said, in a loud foghorn voice, "Sign my tits." Taken aback, but amused, Lance scrawled his name across her chest and then painted her erect nipples. The audience broke into hand claps, catcalls, and invitations to hook up with them after the concert. The young and slim wanted to ride the youngest, biggest, maddest bull they could find. Older female lechers, whose bodies sagged in all the usual places, wanted a gentler bucking and fucking interlude.

The young, aggressive, and dedicated horn-toads in the audience spontaneously stood up, bared their succulent, bouncy and hard up-pointed boobs, and chanted "sign mine too." There was five minutes of mayhem. The band broke into a fast, hot, loud number attempting to bring things under control. They did it. Eventually.

At one performance, Lance went into the musicians' waiting room, fired up his pot pipe, and took a big drag, sucking the blueish nectar deep into his lungs. He let the smoke sit for a while, making sure that his tissues were saturated. Then he slowly blew out curlicues and eddies of sweet-smelling mist, and was transported into a mellow world where everything was calm, quiet and released him from his frequent anxiety and anger.

The phone rang. *Fuck*, Lance thought, *I really don't want to talk to anyone. Too tired.* The noise assaulted his space, his desire to be alone. It bloated an already intense hangover headache. Lance tried to ignore the phone. After fifteen or twenty rings, he stomped across the room, lifted the handset on the instrument of misery, and slammed it down, ending the call, and went back to his reading.

The phone rang again and continued to ring for a good three minutes. He spurted, *Jesus Christ almighty. Too much. Maybe someone's going to give me a million dollars. Fat chance.* Lance got up, stomped to the phone, and picked it up as if it were a weaving cobra ready to strike. He brusquely said, "Yes. What? Who are you?"

"It's Gil Evans, Lance. You in a bad mood or something?"

"Sorry to be so gruff. I didn't get home from a jam until six this morning, and I'm a little fried. What's up?"

"I want to talk to you about playing with my new big band." Lance's heart pumped like a fire engine's hose at a blaze. He became hyper-alert as Evans said, "I'm going to record modern. Heard you play at the jam session at Cannonball Adderley's and a couple of other places, but I don't remember where. You have the fantastic cool sound, remarkable speed, and articulation that I need."

Lance's pulse shot up with the prospect of playing with Evans who was thought to be one of the era's top jazz composers.

"So, what's it all about?"

"It's going to be called *Beyond Cool*. My previous album, *Gil Evans Plus Ten*, was a conventional treatment of old standard ballads and jazz pieces. *Cool* is avant-garde. I think it will push jazz into new dimensions—structure, voicings, and rhythms. I've been influenced by lot of classical composers, particularly impressionists like Debussy, Satie, and some of the moderns like Messiaen and Stravinsky. There's plenty of room for trumpet improvisation."

"I picked instruments with different timbres—the tone and color of the instrument in each tier. This mix makes for a rich and unique sound. It also allows me to double-up on phrases and melody lines, one from the upper tier and one from the lower. I throw in a few twelve-tone parts to make the chord structure more interesting."

Lance said, "Not quite sure how this works, but I guess I'll find out. Who's playing?"

"You'll know them all. They're the best of the best. To name a few cats, there will be Gerry Mulligan on baritone sax, Max Roach on drums, J. Johnson on trombone, and John Lewis on piano."

"I thought that Lewis only played with his own group, The Modern Jazz Quartet."

"No, I begged him to do this one gig. He owes me a couple for doing some original charts for the MJQ. He has such subtle touch and matchless finesse, that he was the only one for the job as far as I was concerned."

"Sounds like a stellar cast. What's next?"

"We have seven concert dates, starting in the City and concluding in L.A. We'll be on the road for about two and a half weeks. I'll give everyone the scheduled dates and venues at the first rehearsal. Here's the rehearsal schedule: One week of rehearsals starting on April 10th. Can you make them?"

"Sure. Can't wait. And thank you for the honor of playing with you. It will be a real boost for my career."

"Great, I'll see you at Empire Rehearsal Studios on West 43rd street at 1:00 PM on April 10th."

Trying not to appear too excited, Lance said, "Thanks for the opportunity. I'll see you there."

6
The Studio

AFTER THREE DAYS OF rehearsals, the finely-honed band was ready to lay down Cool Blues. Lance's destination was the Empire Rehearsal Studio. It was housed on the second floor of a late 19th century four-story brick office building on West 44th street, and two blocks west of Times Square—close to the center of the music industry's action. Producers, artists, recording studios, agents, entertainment lawyers, theater owners, and record labels had offices strewn around the area.

Lance exited the subway at the south end of Times Square at about 12:00 PM and walked north toward 44th Street. He was greeted by the agglomerated sounds of taxis, cars, and busses laying on their horns. One taxi driver, hemmed to the curb by another, blasted his horn and gave his nemesis a pumped fist. The other leaned out his window and said, "Fuck you, asshole." Office workers, men in dark suits and Fedoras, and women in long tapered dresses and fancy hats scurried along the sidewalks on their way to lunch. Tourists craned their necks to look at the buildings, signs, and glitz. It was a pickpocket's delight. The air was choking with exhaust and diesel fumes.

What a mess, he thought. *Used to be an exciting place, now, at night it's scary—pimps, whores, peep shows, a few restaurants and diners, and jammed with cars. The theaters have been falling apart since the '30s. Not very safe at night. At least the big movie houses are still running.* Lance walked by huge marquees screaming: "Elvis Presley, *Love Me Tender*"; "Samuel Goldman's *Porgy and Bess*"; "*A Night in The City*, starring Richard Widmark and Gene Tierney"; "Desi Arnez and Lucille Ball Live." At night, he knew that the huge advertising signs—for Camels, Coca Cola, Planters Peanuts, Admiral Appliances, Canadian Club Whiskey, and a raft of others, would

The Studio

be working their magic; swirling and flashing in a rainbow of neon colors pleading, "Buy me, buy me."

Lance met Lee Konitz in front of the studio. The studio was in a turn-of-the-century, four-story brick office building that was the worse for wear. They chatted about the current jazz scene, particularly the newcomers, and who was appearing where. They climbed up the stairs, consciously avoiding the rickety and unreliable brass and steel cage elevator. The entered the studio's large reception room that served as a warm-up room and a place to dump empty cases, and were greeted with the cacophony of instruments warming up.

Everyone was a bit nervous, which would seem odd for performers who played in public night after night after night. But recording is different. It's as if their souls were to be captured in vinyl for the entire world to see and judge. And if any one musician was not dead-on with their music, the world would see a diminished or tattered soul.

After a, round of greetings, the members of the nonet went into the studio.

Gil Evans was in the control booth conferring with the recording engineer and producer, Al Bernstein from Blue Note records. They were gesticulating with rapid arm movements and pointing at parts of the eight-foot-long control module, which balanced the volume and frequency (bass and treble) of each of the three incoming record tracks and equalized the signals-balance of each input. The recording engineer was placing the microphones so that each group of instruments would be appropriately recorded for later mixing into the final master, which would be used to manufacture records for distribution.

Evans entered the studio and greeted the group. He said, "We've got the best of the best jazzmen here. This will be an outstanding album, a pace setter, an original hormonal confection. The first recording will be "Rain." Lance, you have a lot of solo work on the album. Play dark and a bit musty." Evans checked with the booth, got an OK that they were ready to record, and gave the downbeat.

One week later, the recording engineer, Evans, and Bernstein, the producer, supervised and approved the final mixed tape. Six weeks after that, the album *Cool Blues* was released. The critics' reviews were more than anyone could expect from a new sound, modernistic treatment of jazz.

Downbeat Magazine said:

> Cool Blues *takes a new direction in modern jazz. Evan's intriguing nonet brings a classical tint into the jazz world. He uses traditional sextet orchestration plus French horn, flute, and tuba. Adding these instruments allows a new modal form—a variation of scales, chords, and texture never used before in jazz. His compositional innovation will provoke changes in the jazz scene as did Stravinsky for classical music. Lance Williams delivered a remarkable performance. His dark and plaintive solo on "Rain" set a pungent mood for the entire album. His voice is unique. Some say he sounds like Miles, others, Clifford Brown. We disagree. While his technique is as good as Brownie's, his elegant phrasing and solo technique are singular. Lance Williams is one to watch. He's arrived as a top-flight trumpeter on the modern jazz scene.*

For Lance, it was all up from here. He was one of the big boys now.

7

Improvisation

LANCE STROLLED DOWN TO Cooper Square in the Bowery on his way to play at the Five Spot on St. Mark's Square in the East Village, another club that sprouted musicians such as Coltrane and Charlie Mingus. Dilapidated red brick tenements lined the street. Rusty fire escapes zigzagged down the facades of the buildings. Chunks of mortar and loose brick fallen from the buildings littered the street's gutter where they had been kicked off the crumbling sidewalk.

The buildings were stacked tightly next to each another. The High Spot's rooms had little light or ventilation except for those facing the street. Rats would skitter over feet, and other creepy-crawly vermin, including fleets of cockroaches that would speed away when lights were turned on. The tenements were for the poor and immigrants who had hopes for moving out of poverty into a better life. That would happen for a few, but it would take the next generation to take significant steps upward in the world.

The Village was also a haven for beatniks, poets, artists, poor whites and a large colony of immigrants in their own cloistered neighborhoods—Irish, Italian, and Eastern European Jews. There were few blacks. It was basically for the working class, for those who had work.

On this balmy starlit night, Lance was playing with Charlie Mingus's quintet. The Five Spot was one of the few clubs that booked and helped up-and-coming jazz groups and musicians, including Mingus, Ornette Coleman, Thelonious Monk, and Eric Dolphy. Mingus was an avant-garde composer and bassist. He brought in a top-flight quintet fronted by Coltrane and Lance. The group had just finished playing the last number in the set—Mingus's hard bop fast tune, "Straight No Chaser." Sweaty from the hot stage lights, Lance put his very expensive custom horn in a blue-velvet-lined case, placed his mouthpiece and mutes in special compartments, and put a protective cloth over the instrument. He was exiting the club when a boy, who by law shouldn't be in a club that served alcohol, walked up and tapped him on the shoulder. Lance abruptly stopped and turned to look at the boy who said, "My name is Richard. Please Mr. Williams, would you show me how to improvise? I'm a great jazzman, and can sight-read like a demon. But I'm terrible at improvisation."

Lance glared angrily at the kid and snapped "Go away kid. Go back to your high school band teacher. He gets paid for teaching you."

"But he doesn't know jazz."

Lance said, "Tough," and started to walk away. Then, mellowed by a healthy dose of pot, he had a rare moment of introspection and empathy. He remembered all the encouragement and mentoring by local teachers and musicians when he was in high school. His ego and motivation were boosted by fans who cheered him on, and by help from some of the great jazzmen in New York. He thought: *What the hell, people were good to me, maybe I should return the favor this once.* He took the kid into the warm-up room which had a piano.

Lance started by saying, "Richard, a few lucky musicians are wired for improvisation. They intuitively hear the chords and rhythm and invent their own music around them. Like the great artists Picasso and Rembrandt, who had brilliant visual insights, and were wired for art. You're not a natural, but you can learn enough to be competent and play with some pretty good local groups."

Richard said, "Are you sure that I can learn?"

"Yes, if you listen to the great improvisers, and practice, practice, practice. Learn their licks and then try your ideas out with a small band. You can copy their licks, those set phrases or embellishments that you'll play to make a transition from one part of a tune to another, or to add spice anywhere in a piece. And you'll begin to develop your own improvisation style."

"Do you think I'll make it?"

"Don't know. It's a lot of work. Are you willing to practice at least three hours each day?"

"Yes, for sure."

"If that doesn't make you a first-class improviser, then get into a big band. They usually have one or two trumpets that improvise well. But if your improvs are just good, but not top-notch, you'll get the nod for a few solos but you can help drive the band. If you play as you say, you might be a prime prospect for a good band and studio work. You'll be playing a lot of tunes for the first time in concerts and studios. You'll have to play perfectly on the first time you've seen the charts.

"Man, you listened to Coltrane and me tonight. Coltrane's one of the best improvisers around, and I'm right up there with the top. It's all about getting inside the music. You, the music, and your horn become one. Listen to some of Stan Kenton's bands. He had a screamer, Maynard Ferguson, who took the horn way beyond the upper range that it was designed for. Conte Condoli had a fine, smooth sound. but improvisation is different. You have to lose yourself in the music. Take your music into a free space; play inside the basic structure of the tune. Here's part of a story by from the *New Yorker* by Alec Wilder that's making the rounds. Scan it.

You listen to the basic signals that you get from the music—forms, chord structures and rhythmic cycles that are basically carriers of the fundamental signals that you get. You dialog with the music and hear where it's going—what a musician's definition of the current situation and sometimes it's possible futures.

Richard took a minute to look at the article.

"I still don't get it. What he says is confusing, too general. I don't understand what he's saying."

"Let me give it another try. Improvisation is from the heart, not your head. You're playing in a space, bound only by the basic structure of the tunes—the rhythm, chord structure, pace, and your imagination. You can develop your own licks.

"Think of it this way: you're on a bicycle chained to a stake in the ground. Around the stake is the melody. You take your basic direction from these. But the chain is long, and you can venture far and rhythm out from the stake in your own free space. You can head straight out from the stake with a straightforward interpretation, or you can wander all over the circle formed by the extended chain. Sooner or later, you'll hit the edge of the musical chain. Don't go farther. If you do, you'll be playing garbage."

"Wow! Who do I listen to"?

"Gerry Mulligan is good and effective straightforward improviser. He moves straight out to the end of the chain. Linear. But the baritone sax is cumbersome; limited in the speed that you can play and its tonal range. Or you can ramble through the circle, and do anything that you want. Go out

IMPROVISATION

as far the chain allows. Explore all the free space. Freddie Hubbard, who Diz mentored, plays the lowest and highest notes possible, with intricate runs, embellishments, and beyond rapid-tonguing. He's all over the map when he improvises. But as soon as you start to go out of the basic structure, the chain reaches its limits and pulls you back into the space allowed by the tune. In other words, you can do anything that you want, but don't go beyond the chin's circumference. If you do, you'll be playing garbage."

"Who's good at it?

"Two of the greatest trumpet improvisers are Clifford Brown and Dizzy Gillespie. Two of the best sax men are Coltrane, who you just heard and, of course, Charlie Parker. Listen to Diz and Freddie Hubbard. They suck up all the free space available. Listen to them and practice, practice. The basic trumpet skills—scales, tonguing, and tough exercises—are key to building your skills. Go back to the Arban Method. It was first published in 1859, and is still used by many starting and expert trumpet players. It will take you from basic to very advanced exercises and classical pieces. Then listen to great jazz. Recreate what the soloist is doing and then make up your own licks—your own embroidery on the tune. If you're not practicing two or three hours a day, forget your dreams and stick to your high school ensemble."

Lance put a Lee Morgan recording on a dusty old LP player. "Listen to the notes. Da da da da de de da de tu tu tut." Lance handed Richard his horn.

"You'll let me play your gig horn?"

Lance managed a weak smile and said, "Sure, but if you screw it up, the broken horn monster will come and ruin your lip forever. I'll put the tune back on and you play Hubbard's solo."

Richard put the horn to his lips and did a passable job of playing the introductory melody. But when his turn came to recreate Morgan's solo, he went off into outer space—bobbled notes, erratic runs, and off-key moments.

"Man, you really broke the circle. The music god will piss on you if you keep up that shit. I can recommend a couple of books like *The Jazz Method for Trumpet* that contain transcriptions of the greats that you can follow and put your own twists on. If you want to go further, go to George Smithfield for lessons. He's the best. Aside from practice, get out there and find the best amateur bands that will have you. Blow them as far around the circle as you can."

"If I come to another gig of yours, will you tell me how I'm doing?"

"Naw," Lance said thinking, *I don't what want to waste my time on this kid. Or any other for that matter. I guess I was feeling so good after the gig that I lost my judgment.*

Richard walked out of the club conflicted. He was inspired and elated by having Lance, this famous person, help him. But his face showed otherwise. It drooped with downturned lips and eyes that looked down at the sidewalk as he slowly walked away from the Five Spot. He looked depressed. He wasn't a natural.

Lance exited, immediately purging Richard from his mind, and headed off to a 2:00 AM jam session at Bud Powell's place.

8
The Interview

DOWNBEAT MAGAZINE REPORTER, Frank Dunphy, met with his editor, George Hardcastle, to discuss his upcoming interview with the star jazz trumpeter, Lance Williams. Hardcastle said:

"I want to review the list of basic topics that we agreed you'll cover with Lance. Beyond these points, use your considerable interviewing skills to delve into other issues as they arise or that you think of during your session."

Frank handed George a piece of paper and said: "This is my outline:"

- General take on today's jazz scene
- Who's he playing with now?
- Why does he play jazz? What motivates him?
- His reputation as an arrogant, pugnacious, confrontational guy.
- How he feels he stacks up with the other greats.
- Who are his heroes and why?
- What trajectory does he see for himself in the next three or so years?

"Any changes you'd like to make?"
"No. Need your article two weeks from today."

George added that this would be one of a handful of in-depth profiles featured in the Newport Jazz Festival issue to be released in July, a month before the August event. "Make it your best." Frank called Williams and made an interview appointment for the following week.

Dunphy took the subway to 142nd Street and Lenox Avenue in lower Harlem and wandered up to the High Note Bar and Grill to meet Williams. About fifteen minutes early for the session, Dunphy walked up to

THE INTERVIEW

the entrance to the bar. He automatically sucked in the details of the place with his writer-reporter's eye, and almost photographic memory. *This man will be the equal of the top guys—Miles, Brownie, Freddy Hubbard, and Diz, and a future Hall of Famer. He's a first-rate SOB-asshole-narcissist and his drive be the best, the greatest horn on earth, draws him to publicity like a starved lion to prey. I don't like him and this may be a very difficult interview.*

Outside, the bar looked like any other dive in the neighborhood except it was marked by a large neon eighth-note in the window, and a canopy that said "High Note" on one side and "Music Inside" on the other. As Dunphy entered the space, he recalled that many a fine player was discovered during the club's Friday night showcase of up-and-coming jazz musicians and groups. Agents and A&R men (Artist and Recording people from record labels) flocked to the sessions hoping to find the next great jazzman climbing up the ladder. Often, after-hours jam sessions were hosted by "made" musicians with some of the best young players in town. The sessions usually started about one or two in the morning after most musicians had finished their regular gigs. In the early morning, the men went home to sleep, or play in a studio session.

The inside of the space was, for the most part, just a plain, ordinary, sort of worn, but comfortable drinking hangout. Part of the neighborhood's history. There were the expected booths lining one side of the room opposite the mahogany bar. On the walls, there was a photo gallery with signed pictures of many of the era's greatest jazzmen. At one end of the spacious room, there was a small bandstand where selected jazz groups could bring their band for an outing. There were forty small black tables, each with a candle, ashtray, and a fake red rose in a tiny vase. The food was simple—burgers and fries, steak, ribs, and soul food including crispy southern fried chicken, chicken fried steak with collard greens, sowbelly, sweet potatoes, and corn bread. The cook was a middle-aged black man from Tennessee, who really knew how to cook soul food.

Seated at the bar was a black couple, maybe in their fifties. The man was dressed in a black turtleneck, black pants and black suede shoes. All was topped by black porkpie hat with a single raven's feather sticking out from the band around the crown. Maybe a cool dude wearing the latest jazz garb. Maybe a jazz spectator. Maybe just out for midday drink with his woman. The man looked sad and depressed. He was doing whisky shots chased by a Pabst.

The woman was wearing one of the more up-tempo and expensive casual outfits common in the black, upscale, Harlem community. She was dressed in flaming red, with a broad-brimmed black hat. The red hatband glittered with a galaxy of rhinestones and the hat was capped with a large red feather gleaned from some unfortunate tropical bird. A broad black belt, with a red cloth buckle cinched her slender waist, and black silk slacks tapered to about eight inches above her ankles. Her red flats were liberally sprinkled with shining black dots. She was drinking a straight-up chilled martini, and drizzles of condensation streamed down the side of her cold glass. She looked angry. Both were staring into their drinks, saying nothing to each other—like a long-married couple who were bored with their relationship and had, long ago, said all that they had to say to each other. There were a few other patrons at the bar who looked like they lived for booze. Dunphy settled in a secluded back booth, ordered beer, and waited for his quarry.

Lance entered the High Note backlit by the bright ten o'clock sun spilling through the door and windows. To Dunphy, he appeared as sharp black silhouette. His features were dark and unreadable. But the reporter recognized his tall shape and hurried walk, and rose to meet him. He could now see Lance's face with its intense "get the hell out of my way, fuck-you" look. Lance slid into the booth and ordered a beer.

"Lance, great to see you again, thanks for the interview. I hear that you had a great gig at Birdland last night."

Frank took out a steno pad, ready to take notes in his almost illegible handwriting that only he and a secretary could decipher.

"Man, we were groovin' We had some of the usual suspects on the stand: Philly Joe Jones on drums, me on trumpet, Coltrane on tenor and soprano sax, Paul Chambers on bass, and Bud Powell on piano. A delight. We've been together enough so that we knew how each of us plays, can anticipate each other's moves. The band moved as one, like a flight of birds headed north for the winter."

"Stellar group."

"Yeah"

"So, tell me what's going on in the jazz scene now?"

"You're the reporter. You tell me."

"Come on Lance, that's a simple question."

THE INTERVIEW

"Well a hell of a lot's changing fast. Jazz is in now. It's drawing all kinds of people. The fans are young, maybe 20 to 40 with an older group that grew up with the Chicago-New Orleans style, were immersed the swing era, and naturally gravitated to modern jazz. We have some pretty far-out sounds pushing the scene forward. Mingus, Archie Shepp, and Sun Ra are often into the dissonant; use strange chords and rhythms and free-form improvisation. Wild stuff. The celebs love it. Frank Sinatra, Mayor Wagner, and Desi and Lucille were at the gig last night, and even Eleanor Roosevelt stopped in to get the vibes."

"How do you rank yourself among the ranks of fine trumpet players?"

"You had to ask? Where you been man? I'm absolutely at the top."

"But everyone can't be at the top. How are you different from the rest of the stellar players?"

"That's a tough question. It's hard to define. Each of us has an unmistakable sound drawn from experience, practice, and feeding off each when we listen to or play with others. You'll hear the difference when you listen to us play. We each produce a sound and style distinct from the others, and we're the best in the country, if not the world, in what we do. We intuitively make sure that we're different in a meaningful and emotional way. The sounds differ from a complex mixture of tone, speed, articulation, feelings. It takes years to develop your style."

"Changing the subject, why do you play?"

"What the hell do you mean by that? I play because I love to play."

"There must be some basic reason why you play."

"I want to express myself, uniquely interpret songs, try new things and grow my skills. I want to enter my audience's heads, hearts, and guts. I tell a story. I'll do whatever it takes to get my version of the song's message across. I set a mood for each piece: delight, happiness, anger, solitude, romance, or darkness."

"So, how has your playing changed since you entered the New York scene?"

"A lot, man." Haven't you listened to me play? If you don't change and move your art forward, you go backwards. You fade."

"How have you changed?

"I now have a rounder, darker sound. I'm playing with new and different chord changes and progressions for lot of the tunes that I play. My runs and intervals are faster, more distinct, and I've added some new licks that work well. My music is simpler but more complex and graceful, if that makes any sense to you. Someone said that I play exquisite sheets of sound like an unrelenting waterfall. Better than Brownie, the current 'note king.'"

Lance spaced out and watched the couple at the bar leave. Just a break in the conversation, a rest from words.

Frank said, "Come back to me Lance. Are you satisfied with your playing now?"

"Of course not. You have to reinvent, reinvent, and reinvent; stay well ahead of the game; contribute new stuff to the jazz community."

Frank pressed on: "Some say that you are hard to get along with, and a bit moody and quick to jump on somebody of something that displeases you. I heard that you had a row with Quincy Jones."

"Yeah, that was too bad. I didn't like the tempo that Quincy used on "Watermelon Man." I was a little pissed about something, so I took it out on the great man. I guess I said something like, 'Asshole, this sounds like a street corner Salvation Army band in a blizzard—sloppy, wrong tempo, and the chord changes at numbers 67 to 101 on the chart are ratty. I think that you ought to do this…' At that point, Quincy, usually a gentleman, stuck his nose in my face and said something like, 'This is the way it's going to be played. If you don't like it, I'll get someone else to play for the next session.' I backed off, not that I was wrong—I was dead right as usual—but it was politic to drop the subject. It's ironic that after the session ended and we had calmed down, we discussed the changes that I suggested for the piece, and Quincy used them. I don't suffer fools lightly and get royally pissed when someone screws up, or the music simply doesn't work well."

Lance changed the subject. "So, Frank, what are you working on?"

"Well, we've got the thrash of the Newport Jazz Festival coming up. We have every reporter, plus some stringers covering the music, the festival in general, and developing profiles and commentary on a bunch of players. The entire July book will be about the festival. We're doing a feature on a newly steamrolling, aggressive Count Basie. And Lance, your quintet is one of the headliners. There'll be a ton of other talent including The Thad Jones Big Band, Stephan Grapelli on violin, Wayne Shorter, Eric Dolphy, and Miles, and lots of other first-rate acts. Old Fort Adams will be hotter than hell—the temperature and the music. It's going to be a gas. I've been assigned to cover Basie as well. What do you see in the future for you?"

Lance smiled. "Still on top. I'm going to do a lot more composition. I'll continue heading my own group. Certainly a quintet, and a maybe a larger group like Evans used on *Porgy and Bess* featuring Miles.

"Style?"

"Way out there."

Lance abruptly stood up and said, "So Frank, gotta wrap this up. Have to go to a recording date. Bye."

As Lance wandered out, Dunphy thought, *and maybe a hit of heroin to get "up" for the take.*

9
MINGUS AND LANCE

LANCE'S PHONE JANGLED HIM out of a deep sleep. He'd been at a jam session until 4:00 AM, and the last thing he wanted to do was talk to somebody. He picked up the phone and said, with obvious disdain and annoyance. "Who is it? What's so fucking important to bother me at this ridiculous hour?"

"Mingus," was the reply. He barreled on and tersely said in his gravelly voice, "I want to see you. Now! I live in the Village at 223 West 3rd street." Mingus abruptly hung up."

Lance thought, *barely know the guy. Played as a substitute on one of his gigs at the Blue Note. Went OK, but he's rough on his men. And the most egocentric and bizarre bastard I know. Almost as abusive as Miles. Not as bad as Miles I think. I'll see.*

Nobody turned Mingus down, so Lance scurried to Mingus's Village apartment, not having a clue what he wanted. And he was confident that whatever it was, he'd blow Mingus out of the water. *After all,* he thought, *it won't be long before I knock Miles off his perch.*

Charlie Mingus, a prodigy bassist and stellar piano player, was considered the greatest jazz composer of his era. He played his bass almost like a violin. He was that facile. His tone was rich. His fingers rippled over the strings like a hummingbird's wings in flight. To add to his formidable talents, he played the piano well enough to perform in excellent jazz groups. His bands perpetually topped many polls including the prestigious *Downbeat Magazine's*. He was showered with honors including a Guggenheim Fellowship, and four Grammy's.

His brilliant works were built on a legacy of blues, bebop, early 50s jazz, Chicago style, and classics from Beethoven to Stravinsky. His gospel roots blossomed when he was forced to go to his mother's church every Sunday. He was wired for music.

Mingus's pioneering style and compositions were completely original and way beyond anything else being composed in the '50s. Many considered him the greatest jazz composer of the era. He was to jazz as innovators such as John Cage, Stravinsky, and Mahler were to classical music. All of them upset and drastically influenced the direction of their musical world. Mingus's style was sometimes dissonant, and atonal, with multiple rhythms, competing chords, and wild flights of fancy. But he left immense space for improvisation.

Newsweek described his personality in 1956:

> *Mingus is an angry man, sensitive about his color, and the fact that his skin was "high yellow" only makes him more incensed about being a Negro. He broods, he gulps red wine by the gallon. He brawls in bars, is perpetually bitter, usually unkempt, and rages against racial discrimination and society in general. To him, the word jazz meant discrimination, second-class citizenship, the back-of-the bus-bit. A former mental patient at Manhattan's Bellevue hospital, Mingus tells anyone willing to listen, "They say I'm crazy, and I really am."*

Mingus's workshops were legendary. Musicians practically broke down his door to get into one. For the players, it was like getting a graduate degree in jazz. In concert, he always played a few of his old standards but concentrated on new experimental works. Sometimes, when the band made mistakes or played sloppily, he would fling a few choice words at the band, and abruptly stop playing in front of an audience. Mingus would then rehearse the offending part of the tune that was screwed up until he was satisfied with the result. Sometimes, without warning, he would throw a curve ball, and invent a tune on the spot. He'd play the theme and rhythm on the piano. Then, Mingus would ask the band to play it—cold, without rehearsal, and with no sheet music.

Mingus's current workshop featured eight of the finest musicians around, including Jacky Byrd on piano; Eric Dolphy on alto, bass clarinet, and flute; and Clifford Jordan on tenor. Lonnie Hillier, his current trumpet player, had dropped out of the ensemble, and his immediate thought for a replacement was Lance Williams.

Lance took the subway down to the Village's Bohemian section, and walked a few short blocks to Mingus's place. He carried his horn in his gig bag in case Mingus wanted him to play a few tunes. After climbing up two flights of stairs, he knocked on the door to apartment 22.

A very fat and rumpled Mingus ushered Lance into his modern duplex apartment. The walls were white and covered with posters of Mingus's appearances; plaques with his mounted gold and platinum records, and framed honors that he had received from various organizations. One of his prized possessions was the Key to the City that Mayor Robert Wagner presented to him. Though Mingus was not prone to sentimentality, it fed his well-developed ego and made him feel part of the greater New York scene—and an even greater man.

Mingus brusquely almost ordered Lance to sit down. "Wanna a drink or some of my Mexican gold? Just fired up a joint. Like smoking silk with a kick. It comes on quick and hot, man. Have some?"

Lance said, "A beer is fine. Just want to chase the hangover away after the jam session at Cannonball's."

"Who was there?"

"Lennie Tristano and Dexter Gordon were there blowing some really odd stuff. Felt like I was in a ice machine with Diz, Rollins, Art Farmer, and Jimmy Knepper, and whirred into some of the oddest sounds and licks you ever heard."

"Good group, but I don't care much for Gordon. Too retro. Too conventional. Knepper, really fucked up during a recording session with me. Totally missed the chord progressions in "Pork Pie Hat." Then, he knocked over his music stand and light with his trombone slide, strewing music all over the place. Almost took the heads off half of the sax section. So, I hit him in the mouth. He's a little pissed at me, but playing OK anyway. I'm going to pay for the best dentist around to straighten his mouth back to where it belongs. Never, ever screw the pooch on my turf or you're going to catch a rain of hellfire."

"So much for the bullshit," Mingus said, pulling on his joint, the fringe of the blue cloud that he exhaled hitting Lance in the face. Lance turned his head away and coughed a few times. He stared down at his untouched and now warm beer, edgy, and thought about what might be coming down the pike for him.

Mingus turned to him and said in his pot-fueled, husky voice, "I want you to join my next workshop. The octet will play in Chicago, New York, L.A., Oslo, and Paris. My trumpet player, Lonnie Hillier, is dropping out, and you would be a great replacement."

Lance felt excited, high, ecstatic at garnering one of the most coveted assignments in jazz.

Mingus continued, "You're on top of your game and your style is unique—not a Miles or Diz or Clark Terry imitator. You have a smooth, full, and athletic presentation. You get around the horn faster than anyone except Clifford Brown. You're one of the best in bop and with some of the new cooler stuff that's coming around. You're ready to develop into an even more formidable force. Maybe you'll become a legend like Miles. Lots of space for improvisation in the music. Really far-out stuff. We have advanced ticket sales that will fill three quarters of our venues. Two weeks of rehearsals start on the first of next month."

Lance jumped at the opportunity. "Yes, I'm in." He would have hugged Mingus but the man wasn't the hugging type. It would be like embracing a porcupine in full bloom. "Give me the time and place."

"We'll rehearse in the Carroll Music Studios at 10:00 AM on June 1st."

"I'll be there."

10
Reckoning

LANCE LEFT HIS DINGY studio apartment in the grubby East Village, and headed uptown along 52nd Street on his way to Birdland to play with Charlie Parker's quintet. Now considered one of the top jazz trumpeters in *Downbeat's* poll, he had just taken a heavy dose of almost pure heroin. He was floating in the clouds, invulnerable, omniscient, high as Mount Everest. *I'm cranked, man. Going to wail tonight. Watch out Clifford (Brown) and Dizzy. I can do anything. Twice as fast as you guys, and I'll have the fans on their feet. Bird, I'm going to blast you off the stage. Take that, Parker, you awkward son-of-a bitch.*

Birdland often had a group of celebrities come and take in the music. It was a fashionable place to be seen. It was not uncommon for Frank Sinatra, Gary Cooper, Marlene Dietrich, and Sugar Ray Robson to be in the audience as well as a couple of newspaper and magazine critics. Lance knew that he would have to perform before some very influential people. A sterling performance could lead to lots of work: backup for famous singers, studio gigs, and recordings after he got his own band together.

The club was named after Bird. The dark brown awning over the club's entrance proclaimed in tan letters, "Birdland Jazz Corner of the World." A large poster at the entrance advertised "Charlie 'Bird' Parker. A Jazz Giant. December 1 through December 5."

The last vestiges of light were fading into night, and several fans leaned on the wall at the entrance smoking cigarettes and having an animated conversation, probably about jazz. One was dressed like James Dean in blue jeans and a white T-shirt, with a black leather jacket, unzipped to his waist, and black motorcycle boots, shined to perfection. Two dudes sashayed out of a red, chauffeur-driven fantailed Cadillac convertible. One was dressed in a robin's egg blue suit. The other wore a dazzling red zoot suit with an over-large, avant-garde coat that fell to his knees. He topped off his costume with a red velvet top hat.

The early crowd was inside, waiting, talking, and drinking.

A bit wobbly and spaced out, Lance went through the entrance and was greeted by familiar sights. The sinusoidal bar was packed with those waiting for the show. The main room was papered in a deep baroque-flocked maroon. There was space for two hundred and fifty patrons at table-clothed tables bathed in the warm glow of candles. The large bandstand could accommodate a twenty-five-piece orchestra. The lights were dim to create a romantic, relatively intimate space. Lance went into the green room near the entrance and warmed up before the performance.

The group mounted the stage. Parker, high on heroin, turned up on time—a rare occurrence that was virtually unheard of. With the assembled band on stage, he lifted his horn slightly, and quickly lowered it, signaling the start of his own searing and rapid fire "Ornithology," a piece that showcased Bird's legendary technique. Lances missed the downbeat and the first six measures and with shaky hands, splatted his way into the tune. Bird frowned and shot invisible arrows into Lance's eyes. Lance's playing was erratic. He missed entrances, played wrong notes, and couldn't follow Bird's rapid pace and chord changes.

After the disastrous gig, Parker said, "You're fired. I guarantee you'll get no work until you clean up your act."

Lance thought, *Like you never had a bad night? You're a legendary fuck-up.*

"Get your ass of the stage and out of this place."

"I just had a bad night and I'll bet nobody noticed."

"Horseshit man. Didn't you see that the audience didn't applaud much for your solos? A few people were whispering to each and not about the décor. The *Times* critic stared in amazement. You've got to grow up and learn to handle heroin. Quit taking it like Cheerios."

Lance gave Parker the "Italian chin flip" as he stormed out of the club and said, "Fuck off." Then he went home and shot up again.

11
THE APOLLO THEATER

IT WAS AN AWFUL fight.

Lance opened the door to his apartment, now shared with Novanna, a gorgeous black woman, with a sinuous, sensual, muscled body, a dancer in musicals and very sassy. He was drunk, heroin-ed up, and belligerent as only a man on drugs and drinking at least six snifters of his favorite potion—Courvoisier—can be. He was dangerously despondent. Novanna was drowsily nodding on the couch and had probably just taken a shot of happy juice. Lance shook her awake and said: "You been out of the apartment a lot. Who you been sleeping with, bitch, whore?"

She said, "No one asshole, just you."

Angry and out of control, Lance hit her hard, twice—a left to the right side of her face, a bruising blow to the left—as if she were a punching bag in a boxer's gym. She fell, but broke her fall by hanging onto a coffee table. As she stood up, Novanna whacked him on the head with a heavy ashtray that was sitting on a table next to the couch. Lance staggered back and fell to the floor—weakened, but not seriously hurt. Blood streamed down from his face almost blinding him. It dripped from his chin onto his favorite white Armani shirt.

"Get the fuck out."

When he stood up, she pushed him out through the apartment door so hard that he fell on his ass. Novanna locked all three locks on the door. Lance, now awake and angry, unsteadily got up off the floor. He pounded hard on the door to get back in. Novanna screamed through the door, "Go away, I never want to see you again." Neighbors stuck their heads out of their apartments to see what the ruckus was all about.

Lance pleaded, "Novanna, let me in baby. I didn't mean it. I was just hopped up. Don't know why I said it. Please let me in. I love you. I know that you're faithful."

After ten minutes of pounding and yelling, and no response from Novanna, he left and slowly, unsteadily trudged down the apartment house stairs onto the street. He immediately went to Shorty's Tall Bar—a haven for all-day drunks. He slugged down a couple more snifters of Courvoisier thinking, *I better get the fuck out of here and do something to keep my mind off all of this shit with Novanna. Ellington's playing at the Apollo. Better go and see the show, always super, and see my trumpeter friends Cootie Williams and Thad Jones, stars in Ellington's band. Maybe we can take a hit together and have some fun. A booster shot is definitely in order.*

It was one of those blistering hot August days. Harlem residents crowded on door stoops, complaining about the heat, exchanging gossip, and talking about their woes and delights. Of course, children and grandkids occupied a lot of the air space. Some sadly talked about a person they knew who was recently shot dead. The fire hydrants, opened by the fire department, gushed water through which kids happily ran, drenching themselves and splashing water on other kids and residents. Gangs lingered at corners. The lurking drug dealers plied their trade. Nights like this brought out the worst on the streets. There were police cars, with their lights whirling, parked on every other corner. Just in case.

Lance took the subway to 125th street and 4th Avenue and walked two blocks west to the famed Apollo Theater. It was here that the most famous, the most talented blacks have performed since 1918. *Gotta sit down. Shit, I'm sweating; my muscles feel like frying bacon. No money for more shit. Maybe one of the guys in the band will give me some. Man, this shit will be wearing off soon, and I don't have the money for another hit now. At least the bitch gave me lots of drugs. That's over now. Have to find another sugar baby,*

Lance slid down the front of a chain link fence in front of the theater that blocked off a vacant lot. The space was littered with rubble, beer cans, paper, needles, cardboard boxes, and all of the detritus one found in a crumbling Harlem. He studied the façade of the theater and then looked in both directions to see if there were any gangs, any danger, any cops. There weren't. But to his right sat three other disheveled, sad looking men. One had his head on his knees, and another was nodding off. A third, likely homeless, was drinking from a bottle of the popular cheap high-alcohol drink of the times, Night Train. Lance thought of the poor people who lived in the decimated neighborhood. A bag lady trudged by with her stolen shopping cart holding the sum of her possessions wrapped in plastic bags. Three kids high on something, with their black leather jackets and attitude, strolled past him. They pointed and laughed at him, gave the cutthroat sign with their fingers.

At about 7:00 PM, a disoriented Lance stood up and wandered unsteadily across 125th Street, narrowly dodging yellow cabs, cars, and trucks that swerved around him, angrily blowing their horns. Some with open windows gave him the finger. Taxi drivers bellowed "jerkoff" and worse. The outside of the Apollo, formerly a burlesque hall, was not particularly attractive or in any way notable. It was a rather cobbled-up example of the early 1900s commercial buildings. Large windows punctuated the front, and an articulated classical cornice crowned the building. Lance went to the front of the theater. He stepped up to the art deco steel box office that was architecturally out of place in this 1913 building. He bought the cheapest seats in the back row of the balcony.

Lance walked into the Apollo lobby filled with a milling crowd of patrons. Some black men were dressed in suits and ties, one with a fancy carved cane with a patterned knob on its top. There were a few men in black leather suits and jackets, and others in a mish-mash of casual clothes. A couple of men, likely high society, wore tuxes. The women wore knee length skirts and tops of many colors, often with a flamboyant hat of the latest fashion. The crowd was dotted with white aficionados of jazz. The Apollo was neutral ground, without the usual acrimony between races. Blacks and whites mingled freely. They were there for jazz, and racial boundaries disappeared, at least for the night.

Lance looked around the lobby and thought: *What a place. The black greats played here: The Duke; James Brown, the godfather of soul; Sonny Rollins; and Diz.* Amateur hour (it was really twenty minutes) featured up-and-coming singers, or bands hoping for a break. The "hour" served as a first act to warm up the crowd for the main event. Many a star had been discovered on these nights. Ella Fitzgerald was one of the many.

Cat Anderson, Ellington's star trumpet player, came up to Lance in the foyer and said: "Hi Lance, how's it going?"

"Not so well. Not getting any work."

"I'm sorry. I heard. You were the best. Up there with the greats. You were flying, man."

"I've asked everyone I know about giving me a gig. No luck,"

"You know as well as I do that you're not going to get any work until you get sober and back in shape. And then you have to work with some of the second-tier groups to prove yourself. You'll have to start all over again. Look at George Sempler. Fine alto player. Thought that he played better on drugs. He started making flubs, nodding off, and doing disjointed improvs. He lost the ability to connect and groove with the other musicians he played with. His tone went to hell in a bucket. Began to sound like he was blowing through a garden hose. That bad. He got no jobs from the best bands."

"Come on. I'm not that bad"

"Makes no difference. Until you go through rehab and stay clean, no one's going to even think about you. Go see Clark Terry or Louis Armstrong. They make a point of helping cats on drugs. Think about it."

Cat left. Lance barely heard Cat's admonition. He was beginning to sweat, and soak his shirt in places. There was light pain in his arms and legs. He felt another depression coming on. There were thoughts, sounds, and images dredged from deep memory. He envisioned himself playing Hayden's trumpet concerto with the Buffalo Philharmonic, the prizes that he won, the accolades of admiring crowds, the competitors that he vanquished.

Lance, still stoned, walked across the lobby, eyes fuzzily focused straight ahead. He didn't notice the patrons staring at his disheveled state, his uneven gait, and his drug-induced stupor. He entered the theater, which always buoyed him. Lance thought he heard sounds of the famous jazzmen who unleashed their artistry here years ago. They were crystal clear, as if Lance was in the audience when they played.

The theater looked like a wrinkled grand dame, a beauty showing her age, but still having vestiges of her former beauty. Paint was peeling; once vibrant colors were muted by age; water stains marked the ceiling and walls. But her buoyant personality and her inspiring fundamental elegance showed through her faults. The theater itself was a three-tiered oval-shaped space. Its balcony gracefully curved and focused on a large stage that could accommodate the biggest of jazz groups. A grand roundel, painted with luminous gold animals on light aqua, graced the ceiling. The decoration looked a bit like a hovering spaceship. From it hung a large backlit art deco chandelier, with an imposing abstract star at the end of its fall.

The Basie's eighteen-piece band was filing onto the stage. Some members were chatting or laughing. Others were practicing solos or parts of the charts that they had not mastered. The musicians were dressed in their standard uniform—medium gray suit with white shirts and a black tie. Their stand lights punctuated the dim stage like stars waiting to twinkle. A very sexy and handsome Ellington entered. His wavy black hair was slicked from front to back and looked like a form-fitting helmet. He wore a tux, and flashed his white-toothed smile to the audience as if to say, "Come dance with me, make love to me. Meet me at the stage door after the show, and you'll have a night to remember forever."

The Duke's performance was salutary. Joe Williams sang a sonorous and peppy "Don't Do Nuttin' 'til You Hear from Me." The band offered a sad and rich version of Billy Strayhorn's "Lush Life," and closed with a screaming performance of "Take the A Train."

On his way out, Lance's world began to spin. He leaned against a column to steady himself.

Suddenly, a lone ghost, dressed in a black Batman-type outfit, buzzed the crowd. It had a sharp, long-toothed, spit-drooling death's head, and large blazing red eyes. The phantom flew, at high speed, straight at Lance. It suspended itself at eye level with Lance's, sending red laser-like beams into his eyes, momentarily blinding him. He felt waves of steam-hot heat pass over his face and scalp. The ghost departed, passing through Lance with a frigid wind, leaving him with a cold frost over his entire body that made him shiver uncontrollably. He shrugged off the phenomenon, thinking it part of the deliriums that an addict gets during withdrawal.

Woozy, Lance staggered out of the theater. He found a streetlight pole to hang onto to steady himself. In his head, there was a noise that sounded like a bunch of newborn chicks clicking their way out their shells. Suddenly two tree branches broke through the metal pole and wrapped themselves around him in a vice-like grip, pinning him to the pole in the tightest of leafy grips. He was oblivious to the world and the evil that might befall him from some meandering bunch of street rogues.

12

Overdose

Lance, weak, staggering, and his heroin high wearing off, barely made it up the three flights of stairs to his small, Salvation-Army-furnished, one room studio apartment. His playing was deteriorating. He was missing entries. His improvisations sounded more like a memorized piece than the soaring free-form solos that his fans were accustomed to. He sat on his couch, fired up a rich mix of heroin, and collapsed into a deep sleep. Maybe too deep.

Louis Armstrong and Clark Terry knew that Lance was failing, ruining his career, and made an unannounced morning visit to see if they could persuade him to get into a treatment facility. The door was slightly ajar, an event that one almost never saw in this neighborhood, or anywhere in Manhattan for that matter. Louis knocked hard on the door and yelled in his gravelly voice, "Lance, are you in there?"

No answer.

"Lance, talk to me."

Not a sound.

Clark cautiously opened the door. The air smelled of booze, cigarette smoke, and the stench of decay. Lance was lying face-up on the couch, his feet falling off of one end and his arms arched over his head like the fallen arches of a once magnificent cathedral. His face and chest were covered with vomit. Louis and Clark rushed to his side, carefully walking around the crusting piles of puke on the floor. Clark said, "Christ, he's soaking wet with sweat. Pale as hell. He's barely breathing. And with a wheeze and rattle."

Louis raised one of Lance's eyelids. "His eyes are dilated. We have to get him to a hospital. Call an ambulance."

Overdose

The ambulance announced its arrival, sirens screaming, lights blazing, and horn squawking. There were thumps and grunts as the EMS technicians struggled to get their gurney up the steep, narrow stairs.

"He's a heroin addict," Clark said. "Is it an overdose?".

"Wait until I examine him." A few seconds later, the attendant said, "Definitely an overdose of horse."

Louis added, "God almighty, not another Parker."

The attendants lifted Lance off the sofa and put him face-up onto the gurney. They moved his arms to his side, and inserted an IV with glucose and sodium chloride in a saline solution. An attendant said, "This is meant to increase his energy level, hydrate him, and replace vital electrolytes lost in his vomit and sweat. His pulse is very low. About 40. Like an Olympic marathoner. Obviously not the case. Let's get him into the bus."

The gurney bumped down the stairs like a car on a well-rippled road. Louis and Clark trailed them. Lance was lifted into the ambulance. One attendant rode in the back with Lance and Louis, while Clark rode in the front with the driver.

Once the doors were shut, the attendant yelled, "Hump it Harry. Don't know if this guy's going to make it." The truck took off like a scalded Road Runner making an unheard of thirty miles an hour, but slower on streets blocked with trucks and cars. Clark yelled at the driver as he ran up on a sidewalk, scattering appalled walkers, to get around a backed-up street.

"What the hell you doing man? You'll get us all killed."

"No worries. Do this all the time. Want your buddy to arrive alive. This is a cup of tea. Dented a few trucks and cars in my day. And the red lights? We go through them. Almost clobbered someone in Ferrari yesterday. The idiot tried to gas-it though an intersection that we were crossing. Hit him and left him sputtering in his very fancy wagon. We always have the right of way. The bastards in fancy cars always want to try to beat us. Then I have to take time off from work to testify in the goddamn court case. City always ends up paying a bundle."

The man in back checked to see that the IV drip was running properly, then gave Lance a shot. Louis asked, "What's that you're giving him?"

"Miltown to lightly sedate him so he'll relax a bit and be able to talk to the docs coherently."

The driver barely missed a truck going through an intersection. In the cab, Clark gasped as the wagon screeched to a halt. Louis braced himself for a crash. The attendant said, "Take it easy, we'll be at Bellevue in a couple of minutes".

"Bellevue? Why not Columbia Prez? It's the best."

"That's a good twenty-five minutes up to 169th Street. You want the man dead? Besides, we're required to take our charges to the nearest hospital and that's Bellevue."

Moments later the ambulance pulled up to the Emergency Room at Bellevue Hospital on lower First Avenue. The EMS attendants unloaded Lance, and Emergency Room personnel took him immediately to a stall to be examined. The attending doctor looked him over and tersely said, "Another God-damn drug overdose. They'll never learn. Get him into detox and rehab. You'll need a consent form and a signed statement of his responsibility for any uninsured charges. You can sign the form authorizing treatment as he's unable to do so. Once detoxed, if he wants to get into rehab, you'll need another consent and financial document signed."

Clark told Louis, "We have to be there when he's sober and can understand what deep shit he's in. We'll have to talk him into rehab. We'll simply say that he's not going to get anymore work until he's well off drugs, and that he's losing the respect of the jazz community and his fans."

13

Hospital

LANCE WAS STILL HIGH when he was taken to the drug treatment center. He was put on an examination table, wheezing and choking. After an examination, a doctor took his vital signs. Lance's blood pressure was a low 90/40; his pulse a very low 40, and his temperature slightly elevated at 101°. He threw up; he was sweating; all symptoms of a heroin addict.

"He looks like an OD."

Louis nodded, "Heroin. We found him unconscious. Drug paraphernalia all over the place. Bags of dope as well as pills."

"Did you bring any of his drugs with you?"

"Yes. We figured that you would want them."

"Take them," Clark said, tendering a bunch of glassine envelops filed with white powder and a couple of bottles of pills.

"I'll get these up to the lab." The doctor ordered a nurse and an orderly to take Lance to a detox room, which was within the long-term drug treatment center. They put him in a wheelchair for his trip to sobriety.

A man met them at the door and said, "I'm Jerry Uselman, the director of the center." With a calm, confident smile, he said, "Welcome. From the sign-in I know that you are Louis and Clark, and the patient is Lance Williams. And you are taking the responsibility for his welfare and financial needs?"

"Yes," said Clark

"I was told that you are looking for a program to get him sober and prepare him to go back into the real world and be able to cope with it."

"Right," Clark said.

Jerry continued, "Let's go into our conference room and sign some consent papers. Then I'll run you through the protocol and take you on a tour of the facility."

Louis and Clark, knowing that they would have to pick up the tab for the treatment with the help of Baroness Koenigswarter, a leading patron of the jazz world, told Lance that they or the Baroness would pay the bills and that his treatment would take at least four weeks. Lance barely understood what they said, but signed the documents anyway. Louis told Lance, once again, that he would never again play with a first-rate group until he was sober. They couldn't tell whether Lance heard the message. But that message would be repeated time and time again until Lance digested it. It should be a strong motivation for Lance to get well. Proudly, Jerry took Louis, Clark, and Lance on a tour of the facility.

They entered the main room for extended stay patients. It was a spacious, bright, happy, yellow room with a large communal table for serving meals and for reading, playing cards and games, or chatting with other patients. Jerry said, "Our patients' rooms are just as nice. You won't find better in any reasonably priced facility. Each has two beds. a closet, cabinets for clothes and personal items, and a window. There are always two attendants on duty—a nurse to handle health problems and dispense medication, and an assistant to handle discipline and other issues. It's not like the hyper-luxury, hyper-priced places like California's Malibu Beach Recovery Center. We do as good a job though, we're just not movie-star posh." Lance, uninterested in the tour, spaced out as Louis asked, "What's the treatment regimen?"

"The program takes four weeks. First is detox which lasts four to five days. The first two days are pretty horrific. We have separate rooms set-aside for that. We believe in the 'cold turkey' method. We want residents to feel the extreme pain of withdrawal as part of the deterrent to their getting back to drugs after treatment. It's a noisy, nasty, very painful process: sweats, muscle aches as if in a killer flu, sleepless nights, hallucinations, nausea, and vomiting. We only give patients drugs for anxiety and depression—nothing to ease the pain of detox."

"What else?" Clark asked.

"There is a structured daily schedule tailored to each patient. It starts with breakfast at 7:00 AM and concludes at 8:00 PM. The program is geared, of course, to get the patient sober and help them deal with their individual problems and demons. The core of the program that everyone takes includes a daily meeting with a counselor to deal with the individual issues and concerns, exercise, cognitive therapy with their psychiatrist, free time for socializing and cleaning their rooms, information talks on a wide variety of topics about addiction and recovery, group therapy, and discussion about how to reintegrate into the real world again. There are lots of other activities that appeal to some individuals, such as building relationships, vocational skills, and spiritual counseling. These are integrated into each patient's personalized program."

Jerry handed them a list of core programs and their options.

Clark asked, "How effective is the treatment?"

"The national recidivism rate is 50 percent. Some addicts have to go through the program two or more times to keep sober. We're one of the best and our return rate is 40 percent."

"What's the refrigerator for?"

"We keep lots of snack food around—yogurt, ice cream, health bars, cereal, and various juices. We have to keep the crowd's blood sugar up, or they'll get very cranky. There are three phones for calls that are allowed for one hour just before dinner. We don't encourage people to be in touch with our charges. Relatives can visit twice a week for an hour. The exit door is always locked. No one goes out unless absolutely necessary and then only for medical tests."

Lance began to slide out of his dreamless sedation, passing through an otherworldly twilight zone. Inside, his mind was encased in a luminescent green globe. Flashes of intense multi-colored streaks zipped through the space like burning meteors. Blue amoeba glided through the scene. It was like his own personal Fourth of July. He was a blind embryo swimming in amniotic fluid and trying to grow up and get out. Suddenly, his father snapped into the globe in full-blown Technicolor, stern face rhythmically blushing red. The apparition admonished the ten-year-old for hitting and bloodying another boy's head with a croquet mallet. All the boy did was win the match.

Lance started to come out of his drug induced trance just in time to hear the words "locked up." He jerked upright in his wheelchair, his face drawn, his eyes wide open. He almost fell as he bolted from the chair, yelling, "No fucking way." He hit Jerry's legs hard, sending him sliding with a bruising crash into a floorboard. Clark and Louis tried to grab Lance by the shirttails as he breezed by. They missed, and were left grasping air. Lance sprinted to the metal exit door and attempted to open it. Locked. He pounded on the door yelling: "Mother-fuckers, let me out; let me out."

Jerry, trailed by Louis and Clark ran to Lance and pinned his arms to the door. With almost superhuman, adrenalin-fueled strength, Lance broke loose, not knowing where to go next. A muscle-building male nurse tackled him, brought him to the ground, and pinned him to the floor. An attendant rushed to Lance's side and gave him a large shot of Miltown to calm him down. Subdued, he was taken to his room, laid down on his bed, and he fell into the restless sleep of the tormented.

14

Detox and Recovery

LANCE THRASHED IN HIS sleep; moaning; dreaming of some personal hell. As he awoke, he found himself drenched in sweat. His body was shaking and he ached throughout. And the headache? It felt like all of the horns in the universe blasting whinnies, clucks, and Mahler. It gripped him like the Asian flu on steroids; like spending the night under a pile driver. He threw up all over the bed and himself. He was depressed. He rang the call button for a rehab attendant. When the attendant arrived, Lance was out of bed and sitting on the floor, resting his head on his pulled-up knees—a vertical fetal position—as if he was trying to disappear onto himself. His body shivered, he rocked forward and back. He was pale as a bleached bed sheet and, through a mind-haze, he thought, *Fucking Christ almighty. I'm going to die.*

A doctor came into the room, along with Lance's counselor, Dan, who would deal with his day-to-day issues. Dan, like most of the counselors, was a recovering addict himself, and could empathize with the patients. He knew very well the routine and pitfalls, and could communicate effectively with his patient.

"Am I going to die?" Lance blurted out, fielding a wrinkled sweaty frown and a grim, pained face.

"No. But you're going to feel like this for three or four days. And then the pain will taper off, and a week after that, you'll be out of the woods. You may feel slight withdrawal symptoms and a depression for weeks after treatment."

"What happens now?"

"You'll get regular doses of benzodiazepine to control anxiety, sedate you, and ease the pain of withdrawal. I'll give you your first pill before I leave.

Detox and Recovery

"Three days from now you'll see your psychiatrist and me. Then you'll have four or five days of ever-diminishing symptoms. The shrink will help you discover the underlying causes of your dependency and the triggers in the outside world that could haul you back to heroin. Your counselor will guide you through the process of getting sober and what you must do to say sober. Hungry?"

"No. I still feel like throwing up."

"The vomit impulse will be with you for a while. Anyway, meals will be brought to you during your first three days. After that, you'll eat in the common room with your colleagues."

The doctor gave Lance a benzodiazepine pill and left. Dan gave Lance his daily schedule, and said, "For the next three days, we'll concentrate on getting you through the worst stages of withdrawal. You'll see Dr. Shah, your psychiatrist, several times and me many times during a day. You'll get a lot of exercise which will make you feel better and get a lot of toxins out of your system. After that, your schedule will be full from wake-up at 6:30 AM to lights out at 10:00 PM. In a couple of days, Dr. Shah and I will be meeting with you to identify the triggers that make you want to take smack."

Lance was groggy and slowly being sucked into never-never land.

It wasn't unusual to have a patient spacing out, and Dan would patiently repeat Lance's schedule and would escort him to therapy and other activities until it was engrained in his patient's mind.

"Let me tell you about your routine after the first three days. Your daily schedule will include group therapy, mindfulness training, exercise, vocational skills, and alternative therapies such as yoga, meditation, and massage. As you can see, there are a variety of activities each day. It's very structured. You'll have time to meet the others in rehab. Meeting your colleagues is very important. You need human contact. You'll make good friends. Your peers will tell you about their experiences here, their former life, and what they've learned here and how to cope with the system. They will be a valuable source of support. You'll get into the rhythm of the program quickly."

After several days, Lance's symptoms did lessen, only to be replaced by a depression. Later, on his way to his third session Dr. Shah, he thought, *This shrink stuff is totally unnecessary as far as I'm concerned. I'm very smart and can figure out things for myself. I don't see any breakthroughs that will help me detox. My problem is simple: too much dope. Such horseshit.*

Dr. Shah ushered Lance into his office. The space was designed to project a calm, warm, embracing atmosphere, and relax the patient. There were lots of plants; real wood paneling; a coffee table in front of an attractive, comfortable-looking, soft leather psychiatrist's couch; two generously upholstered chairs; and a large saltwater fish tank filled with colorful topical fish. The fishes' languid movements would calm, even mesmerize, patients who looked at them.

Lance sat down in the plush chair opposite Dr. Shah, who said, "We already know that you're an extraordinary musician. You've made it in a rough and competitive field. Making it from being a provincial player in Buffalo to a star in New York is quite an accomplishment. So, with this success, why would you take up drugs? What happened to drive you into this dead end?"

Lance looked out of a window and thought, *Shit; I know what dumped me into heroin. I'd just gotten off twelve one-night stands. That would exhaust anyone—on the tour bus every night to go to the next venue. We'd stay in just-adequate hotels, get a cheeseburger if there was time, and play. On top of this mess you had to turn in a sterling performance to meet the fans' expectation of excitement and creativity. Then there's Novanna. Bitch. Threw me out of my own place. I went to Miles for suggestions on how to keep from getting "road burn." I didn't know shit about what to do. How to handle anything at that point. I was ripe for any relief. And Miles gave me a way out—heroin.*

Lance bent forward and put his hands over his head so Dr. Shah couldn't see his face. He tried to figure out what caused his fall into the La-La Land of dope. He thought again about the "road burn" incident and decided that the underlying cause was not that. Tears streamed down his cheeks. He stayed that way for minutes. Then, the penny dropped. He lifted his head, shaking slightly, and said, "I'm scared. I'm scared to death that something will happen, and I'll lose everything that I've worked so hard for. Everything."

"So, you're afraid you'll lose everything, but what specifically would cause it?"

Lance went silent for a minute, looked at his hands, and said, "I'll lose my ability to play the trumpet well, or another new player will hit the scene and knock me off the top. Or I'll lose my lip."

"How realistic is that?"

"Not very if I play as well as I did before the dope."

"Well, you're here to learn how to stay off dope. If you do that, what will happen?"

"I'll likely be back on top."

"What happens to musicians when they get on heroin?"

"The lose their edge, start making mistakes, get sloppy about showing up for gigs on time, wear crummy clothes for gigs. Eventually, no one asks them to play."

"If you keep on heroin, what will happen to you?"

"I'll end up dead at 35 like Charlie Parker, or playing trash gigs for the rest of my life."

"So how will you avoid that fate?"

"Stay off dope and keep in good physical condition."

"Right. See you in a few days."

Lance left the appointment buoyed. There was hope. He was confident that, if he could stay sober, he'd be back on top again.

Lance gradually got better. He began to feel like he could remain sober. He was more confident that his music career would burgeon with time. He met and made friends with individuals who shared his problems. He no longer felt alone. Most of all, he had hope. Hope that things would return to normal again. His greatest fear was getting back on drugs.

Two days before his release, Lance sat down with his counselor, Dan, to talk about what he should do when he got back into society. "Lance," Dan said, "now comes the hardest part of your recovery—keeping sober in the world of music which is soaked in drugs. We've discussed this before, but the keys are first, immediately get into Narcotics Anonymous and pick a sponsor who will advise you and give you help on the inevitable days when you're tempted to go for a fix. It's important that you try to find a sponsor in NA who's a musician or from the arts. If you can't, so be it, but such a person will have a very good understanding of where you're coming from."

"I'll do it right away, as soon as I get out."

"You're planning to stay in New York?"

"Of course, that's where my music and life belong."

"I strongly recommend that you *not* stay in New York. We advise many patients not to return to the location, culture, and friends that were part of their drug habit. You'll be returning to the drug-laden musical culture that you came from. The odds of recidivism will be very high once you're back on the New York music scene. You should go back home to Buffalo. Your parents are there, you have friends in the city, and you'll undoubtedly find plenty of opportunities to play." And, with a smile the counselor added, "I don't want to see you here again."

Lance said, "I'll think about Buffalo."

"Keep this in mind. George Carlin once said: 'Just because the monkey's off your back, doesn't mean that the circus has left town.'"

15
Train to Buffalo

THE NEW YORK CENTRAL train wended its way out of the station on its way to Buffalo on a cold winter afternoon. Lance looked at the scenery through the window adjacent to him. He was half present and half not, connected to the outside world and into the interior of his mind. The interior side of his brain obsessed about his situation, his game plan for Buffalo. The outside portion, revealed through his window, let him observe and think about both the urban and country landscapes. The train was sparsely populated, so he had two seats to himself, and could stretch out when he wished, to think or rest. He thought, *Why the hell would anyone who could afford to fly ever take this 12-hour trip?*

As the train lurched over ill-maintained tracks, Lance, thrown from side to side, wobbled down the aisle to the snack bar. He tripped over a passenger's feet in the aisle, and over luggage that had crept out from under the seats. He bounced off the walls when he opened doors between the cars and was jostled when he entered the heaving platform between cars. *Shit*, he thought. *It must be like a "jerk around" ride at a county fair. Hell, I might get seasick if the trip continues this way.* He returned to his seat with acrid black coffee and a slightly stale pastry wrapped in cellophane eons ago.

Lance thought about his friends in New York—Louis, Clark, Max, Coltrane, and a raft of others, his lost reputation, his drug habit, and what awaited him at home—his parents, playing at dances, weddings, parties and other sundry dull and unchallenging events that he thought were beneath him. He'd try to resurrect decades-old friendships and find his musician friends who might give him jobs or network him into the music community to improve his job prospects. Most of all, he needed to join a local Narcotics Anonymous group and get a good and compatible sponsor. He sighed at the very thought of reestablishing himself in Buffalo.

There was about three or four feet of snow on the ground. The terrain was mostly flat. The heads of pussy willows poked through the white blanket like periscopes searching the ocean for a target of opportunity. The multi-colored leaves had long since fallen from the trees, leaving them with shorn branches; stark twisted skeletons. An owl swooped down from its post in a tree, having found a hapless rodent for dinner. Other birds had returned to their sleeping quarters. Night creatures were beginning to stir. Western New York's depressing, daunting winter was here, and would be until April when the spring melt began. It is said that occupants started their heavy drinking in October to ease the pain of winter. Most returned to "regular drinking" along with the spring melt. Lance craved a drink as he mentally dealt with his future. Something to loosen up his thought process, and ease the pain of relocation.

Lance knew that Buffalo would have at least four or five feet of snow. The wind from Lake Erie would be so strong that walkers downtown could be blown off their feet. Ropes were strung in strategic spots to help them stay upright.

Lance recalled playing hockey on frozen quarries. He wasn't much of a hockey player, but it was the thing to do after school, and as much a social event as a hard-played game. He loved to watch professional hockey, even though the Buffalo Bisons were usually near the bottom of the heap. His hero was NHL scoring and assist leader, Gordy Howe, of the Detroit Redwings who led the team in winning four Stanley Cups. He was not called "Mister Hockey" for nothing, and was graceful and tough as nails on the ice. Lance was, however, athletic, and a great backstroke swimmer. He was undefeated in his senior year. Quite an achievement given his dedication to his music.

Lance actually felt excited, an uptick in his mood, as the train pulled into the Buffalo station. He smiled for the first time in the trip. He saw his parents, Sam and Liz, standing on the platform scanning the train windows in hopes of seeing him. *There they are, he thought. Mom's still wearing that old, worn gray winter coat and that damn red hat that should have been retired years ago. A person of habit. Doesn't like to spend money. Dad's wearing that goddamn raccoon coat, his prized possession since his undergraduate days at Hartwick College. Always the rah-rah college kid.*

Lance's mother grabbed him as he got off the train, hugged him, and covered his face with kisses. He laughed and said, "Cut this shit out, Mom, kissing is for girlfriends, not for moms." His father gave him a big bear hug. They departed the station in their spanking new Chevrolet station wagon. A symbol of the times, it had fins and was painted in dark green with a prominent light green swoosh from front to back. They drove to their modest clapboard house, just south of Olmsted-designed Delaware Park.

Lance thought, *Let the games begin.*

16

Home

LANCE TOOK HIS LUGGAGE and horn up to his old room. It was just as he'd left it. Posters of Miles Davis, John Coltrane, Art Farmer, and Maynard Ferguson, among others, decorated the walls. His top-of-the-line Fischer stereo hi-fi outfit was paired with two huge, ear-threatening, parent-assaulting, window-rattling corner speakers. On his music stand was a copy of Gianni's modern and extremely difficult trumpet concerto, and his Arban exercise book, open to the most difficult speed- and tone-building exercises.

He had taken most of his prized collection of discs to New York. Several swimming trophies were on shelves. Clippings about him and his musical achievements graced one wall. His closet was filled with castoff high school clothes. Lance figured that it was about time to get rid of them. That sartorial style disappeared long ago. On his dresser was his senior prom picture with Martha, his high school squeeze. They had both lost their virginity behind the sand-filled beach in Shirkston, across the Peace Bridge in Canada.

Lance put Miles Davis's landmark album, Porgy and Bess, on the turntable. He was flooded with nostalgia. Arranged by Gil Evans, it's a smooth, plaintive, haunting exposition of George Gershwin's famous opera. Listening to Miles brings up my history; frozen in time. I was launched on my way to Juilliard and fame in jazz circles. Now I'm back here starting all over again. Fuck, it's like being a pro golfer who's lost his swing.

He endured a friendly interrogation by his parents about his life in New York—the gigs, what famous people he played with, his drug habit, and what he was going to do now. He mused, Practice and play a lot of local gigs to stay in shape. Return to New York? Probably not. My counselors told me to stay away from the place that got me on drugs, and the City's jazz community is a supermarket for them. My counselor said that, if I went back to the City, there was a 75 percent chance of getting back on drugs.

After dinner, Lance excused himself and told his parents that he was going to Bruckner's Tavern. Bruckner's was the old hangout for him and his high school buddies.

17

BRUCKNER'S

LANCE GOT INTO HIS parents' 1949 Chevy sedan and headed for Bruckner's. He thought, *Maybe I'll see some of my high school friends. I wonder if Bruckner is still serving the underage high school crowd.* He had also invented the Buffalo wing, now served in most of Buffalo's bars and taverns and spreading all over the place. Even some restaurants were carrying the spicy morsels. Bruckner, the fun-loving German owner in his 60s, still held sway at the bar. He overpoured drinks and was loved for it. *Too bad that Bruckner doesn't get a piece of the wing market. Good to be back on an old and familiar turf.*

Lance entered Bruckner's, a typical drinking dive, crowded with a mixed group of patrons, including a young, loud, boisterous squad, probably eighteen to thirty, and a thirty-to-fifties group, a bit more serious and subdued. A bunch of gnarled, blue-collar heavy drinkers and steadies were attached to the bar like a squad of limpets clinging to the hull of a ship. They were intently watching a hard-fought hockey match between the last-place Buffalo Sabres and the Chicago Black Hawks. The home team would get slaughtered, but it was their team and they enthusiastically cheered for it. A Black Hawk high-sticked a Sabre, blooding him and putting him out of the game. Beer bottles rained on the ice. It took ten minutes to clear off the broken glass. The bar fans were sure that the Black Hawks cheated in some unobvious way. Maybe they were on uppers or some other performance-enhancing drug.

Booths lined the wall opposite the mahogany bar. There were tables in the middle of the space between the bar and booths. Neon Schlitz, Pabst Blue Ribbon, and Budweiser signs blared from the mirrors behind the bar. Four tiers of liquor bottles, with many brands of vodka to please the Polish patrons, were stacked beneath the mirrors. Bruckner, a friendly, ruddy-faced man who told raucous dirty jokes, laughed at theirs, and gave advice to his young customers was behind the bar. He had advised decades of students on matters of the heart, parental issues, and how to avoid or deal with their concerns and complaints. He had heard all of the stories before and had ready and time-proved solutions. As was customary, Lance went to the bar to say hi to Bruckner. Seeing Lance coming across the room, Bruckner poured Lance's usual—a Budweiser and a shot of vodka.

"On the house," Bruckner said. "I heard that you were in town. Great to see you back."

"Good to be back. I'm here for the rest of my life."

Bruckner shoved the drink across the bar and said, "Here's your usual."

"Nah, I gave up alcohol and drugs. Killed my music. That's why I'm here—a safer place to live with the support of family and friends and, of course, you and your bar."

"People here much the same as they were when you left. Lots of high school kids and the old regulars who come in to forget some demon, get away from their wives, or drink with friends. Now drink your booze. For old time's sake."

Lance hesitated. All of a sudden, the atmosphere and the warmth of the happy good old days engulfed him. He was hypnotized, fixated on his high school persona, and thought, *Fuck it. Why not have a drink? Regardless of what the counselors said, I can handle it. I can stop whenever I want.*

Lance downed the shot, chased it with beer, and ordered another round to take to a table filled with his buddies. The booths were so high it was difficult to see from one to another. If you turned toward the wall side of the booths, you could get into a date's blouse and up her dress, and she into your pants without being seen by anyone. He remembered the furtive and frequent making out that he and Martha had done there during much of high school. He greeted many of his high school buddies and sat down at a table between Dave and Barry, two former swim teammates. It was like old times.

"Hey, Lance, come sit with us and tell us about your fantastic career in New York."

"Not much to tell. Worked my way up to the top and fell from grace."

"How come?"

"Got into drugs. Couldn't play well anymore."

"Why come back to Buffalo?"

"Back to my roots. Easier to stay off drugs here."

"Well, we do smoke pot—the acceptable mild drug. Great highs. Want to step outside and share a joint?"

"No. That might start me down the drug highway again."

The gang talked about "what we did back then." They bragged about their high school athletic and female conquests. Then about their jobs, wives, girlfriends, and kids. Harry was a newscaster for a local NBC affiliate, and George was a salesman for National Gypsum. They relived the stud keg parties held before each football game—sometimes with grainy 16-mm porn movies obtained from a senior classman who had access to all sorts of shady things. After the bash, most of the guys would head out to find their girlfriends and got into heavy petting.

At one point, Lance spotted Martha in a secluded booth with Gene Masterson, one of the school's studs. The couple was kissing and fondling. Lance still had a big thing for her. Maybe he was still in love at some level. His pulse shot up. Lance made a beeline to the couple, said hello to Gene, and kissed Martha on both cheeks. She blushed with embarrassment; maybe excitement. Gene's eyes, set in a tense, disapproving, drawn face, shot bullets at Lance. Gene's whole persona said, "Get the fuck out of here. She's mine."

Martha said, "How nice to see you." Lance smiled warmly and said, "Me, too." He noted that Martha didn't have a ring on her "married" finger. She was fair game. Lance left, looking back at Martha and she him.

It wasn't long before Gene was dumped and Lance and Martha became an item again. They picked up their romance as if their seven-year separation had never happened.

Martha was not beautiful, but was a rather pleasant, round-faced woman with a "real woman's" body—one with the curves in the right places, with ample and enticing breasts. She wore clothes that emphasized all of her physical assets. Her striking dress included black slacks that were almost too tight, a form-fitting red top, and red flats. No long, flared skirts and dull blouses for her. Her brown hair was crafted into a very fashionable short, pixie-like hairdo, and she always sported a makeup job obviously designed by a professional. She had a slight limp due to a skiing accident in which she had mashed her left leg.

She was smart, and had an outgoing personality that exuded warmth, happiness, and a zest for life. She was so popular with men that she could have worn a garbage bag as a dress and a still attracted a raft of pursuers like moths to a bright light. While each of her features standing alone were just average, her parts taken together yielded a magnetic and striking woman. Except for close friends, many women didn't like her because of her near perfection and ability to attract men. She was just too much competition.

18
Job Hunt

After a couple of days touching base with a lot of friends and nightly attendance at Bruckner's, Lance figured that it was time to get to work. First, he registered with the Musician's Union, which he knew might lead to jobs when bandleaders couldn't find a trumpet player, usually at the last minute. Most of the jobs that came out of the union would be dance bands that mostly played "Boom-Chicka" music, like the omnipresent Lester Lanin orchestra. The simplistic music, the lack of improvisation, the boring charts, the same old songs over and over again were anathema to him. He knew that until his reputation was reestablished, he'd likely be playing a lot of such junk.

One of his best bets was to contact Tony Cavallero, a trumpet-playing friend. He had been playing at jobs in the area since they graduated from high school. Lance was sure that Tony would be of help.

Paul Drew, second-generation Polish and a fine alto sax player, would also be a great connection. In high school, Lance played in Drew's band and Drew played in his. He met with Paul, renewed their friendship, and Paul promised to try and find work for him.

As he worked his way into the Buffalo music scene, Lance made money by playing the usual boring country club, high school, and society dances. Occasionally he got a job with a good jazz-dance group. He played in two excellent big bands and practiced two or three hours a day. He loved Polish weddings, which were always entertaining and lucrative events.

He recalled a Polish wedding reception held at the AFL-CIO union hall. It was a huge wedding and started, as was the Catholic tradition, immediately after noon. Kegs of beer and hard liquor were arrayed along one side of the long, rectangular room. There were the traditional Polish dishes including cold meats, sausage, borsch, breads, herring, and hunter's stew. There were also delectable Polish pastries, but raised chocolate and gingerbread cakes were the favorite desserts. No wonder, Lance thought, all the guests were, to be kind, hefty.

The band consisted of the usual polka band configuration—trumpet, clarinet, drums, tuba, and accordion. The band's job was to keep everyone happy and dancing, or at least stumbling on the dance floor, depending on their state of sobriety. Polish wedding jobs were long and exhausting—maybe six hours—and you could blow your lip into mush at one of these bacchanalian blasts.

Of course, they played polka favorites time after time after time. Favorites were "Roll Out the Barrel," "She's Too Fat for Me," and "Buffaloowski." It took little time at all for the revelers to get schnockered on booze and sweaty from the stream of fast, happy polkas played by the band. The band made good money. Union scale earnings were okay, but the tips they received to play someone's favorite polka were very large and got bigger as the event went on. The usual order of things was for someone to give a gratuity to the band for playing their favorite tune and then stuff money down the front of the bride's dress and dance a polka with her. There was so much drinking at the reception that the band had to stay three drinks behind the guests to have a reasonable chance of finishing the gig.

Spent, Lance rode home with the wedding photographer. He had to stop at the couple's new apartment to take the traditional picture of the groom carrying the bride over the entry door. It was different this time. The short, skeleton-like groom weighed a mere 145 pounds and the bride topped 180. The bride carried the groom over the doorsill.

Once home, Lance thought about Martha as he had done throughout the job. *I have to see her. Now.* Still, he couldn't get New York out of his bones and mind. *And it's said that you can never go back home. Can't recapture your former life.*

19
In Limbo

TOGETHER AFTER THEIR REUNION, Lance and Martha were surrounded by the golden aura of an obsessively in-love couple. They saw each other day and night, excluding everyone else from their life. They made love like newlyweds—anywhere and everywhere. They only had eyes for each other. They went alone to the movies, beach, and restaurants. They reveled in having sex near public places because the risk of being seen was stimulating, erotic. Much to Martha's parents' disgust, they moved into Lance's apartment. Lance's father was pleased with the move, but his mother was her usual disapproving self. They lived like husband and wife, the cozy life that they were meant to have.

But that wasn't to be. Emotional storm clouds gathered on the horizon, threatening their bliss. Lance was conflicted. Should he stay in Buffalo or return to New York?

Alone, Lance went to Bruckner's, which at 2:00 PM was a quiet, comforting place to think about his future and Martha's role in it. As he nursed a beer, long-past high school scenes seeped out of the walls—their first kiss, the proms, when they first made love, the parties, and lots of other memorable events. They had little significance to him now—just distant memories. Lance concluded that staying in Buffalo was not an option. There wouldn't be any decent work for him, no fine musicians of his ilk for comrades, and no musical challenges so he could grow his skills. An absurdly boring, conventional, and unfulfilled life. He would die a bitter, angry man.

If he stayed in Buffalo, there wouldn't be friends that he wanted to share his and Martha's life with. Their high school buddies were there, but they couldn't relate to Lance, who was steeped in his new musical life.

The talk would be about high school days, sports—which Lance could care less about—their kids, and little else. Besides, they were all married, raising families, working challenging jobs, and had little time for Lance and Martha. They weren't interesting anymore, and there were no common interests. There was no choice. Lance had to move back to New York. He was much relieved to have decided, but he didn't quite know how to tell Martha about it.

On a quiet, balmy night with a full moon winking across the water, Lance and Martha settled into a hidden dune at the Shirkston beach. They made love to the point of exhaustion. Lance, uptight and anxious, pulled Martha closer, looking at her with love and hidden apprehension. Heart in hand, and choked up, he said, "Martha, I have to go back to New York. That's where my life is. I can't live anywhere else. I'll rebuild my reputation, and when I have enough money, I'll bring you to New York. We'll start our new life; live together forever." Martha pressed her head into his shoulder and broke into searing, gulping tears. A knife of sad emotion slid into Lance's gut.

Martha tried to quench her tears. After a minute or so, she was able, through her wet sobs, to plaintively whisper, "Why can't we move to New York now?" There was a leaden silence. It took a long time—it seemed like hours, but in reality, it was only a few seconds—before Lance said quietly, "I don't have the money to support us and get an apartment just for the two of us. My early days would be miserable for you. I'll be out every night looking for work, playing, or schmoozing important people in the jazz world. When I get some money and steady gigs, I'll get you up there as fast as a streak of lightning."

During the two weeks before Lance's departure, they cocooned in a surreal world, removed from reality and floating on an embryonic sea of love.

Then the day of departure came.

20

Train to New York

A FORCEFUL, FOREBODING ILL WIND blew Canadian Arctic air over Lake Erie, dumping cold rain onto Buffalo and lowering the spring temperature to an unseasonal 37 degrees. Lance said goodbye to his parents at their house as Martha waited in her car to take him to the train station. When Lance got back into the car, Martha hugged and kissed him as rain pelted the windshield in waves that sounded like a funeral dirge. They drove the ten-minute trip in silence. Lance lightly massaged Martha's neck and she rubbed his thighs.

They hauled Lance's bags and his horn to the ticket window. He bought his one-way ticket to New York, and then they went down to the track where the Grand Central Limited was stationed. The train was scheduled to depart in fifteen minutes. They leaned against a column, welded into one, hugging and kissing and professing how much they loved each other. Lance said, "Martha, I'll love you until the end of time. It won't be long before we're together again in New York."

Lance boarded the train, hauling his suitcase and horn into a train car. He took a window seat next to the platform. Teary-eyed, Martha walked up to his window. They blew kisses to each other and mouthed, "Love you." The train jerked alive and slowly began its long trip to New York.

Lance stared out the window as the train gained speed and watched Martha disappear. The Limited whizzed by Buffalo's industrial mass, then the suburbs, followed by the countryside. The blur of the landscape and the rhythmic click of the train on the track lulled him into a trance-like state.

He envisioned himself walking down the aisle at the Vanguard where Max Roach's quintet was assembled. A yellow spotlight played on Lance as he approached the band. Then, thunderous applause. His fans still loved him. They were happy to have him back. Roach counted off four beats and launched into Lance's showcase piece, "A Night in Tunisia," played at the usual breakneck tempo. He knew that he was back in his rightful place as a star. All was well.

Maybe.

About the Author

C. Davis Fogg was playing classical and jazz music at a professional level in the eighth grade. Panels of music educators judged him to be one of the top student trumpet players in New York State. He was the "go-to" trumpet player for Jazz, Classical music, and solo appearances.

At Yale, he and David Shire formed the Shire-Fogg quintet.

Davis is considered the person that inspired many elementary and high school students to take up a musical instrument.

www.ingramcontent.com/pod-product-compliance
Lightning Source LLC
Chambersburg PA
CBHW071733040426
42446CB00012B/2336